# Manna
# For a Desert of Busyness

Joseph A. Tetlow, S.J.

Sheed & Ward

This book is for Helen Mercedes Tetlow
my mother
who grounded me in world and Word
and then became my friend.

Sheed & Ward™ is a service of National Catholic Reporter Publishing Company, Inc.

Library of Congress Catalog Card Number: 87-63376

ISBN: 1-55612-119-9

Published by: Sheed & Ward
115 E. Armour Blvd. P.O. Box 414292
Kansas City, MO 64141-4292

To order, call: (800) 333-7373

# Contents

# Introduction

The *manna in the desert* fed Israel for forty years, nourishing their bodies into the Promised Land. The *manna* for our spiritual pilgrimage is Sacred Scripture, first of all, wisely portioned out to the whole church through the Sunday readings. But we are given another *manna* in our great tradition of spirituality, and another in the current teaching of theologians and spiritual writers, and yet another in the pastoral instruction of the bishops as they "read the signs of the times." The *manna* of the book's title includes all of these, because the essays start in Scripture and unfold under the instruction of people like Catherine of Siena, Iñigo de Loyola, Pope John XXIII, Karl Rahner, and Ruth Burrows.

Israel's *desert* stretched out to forty years of scorching sand and scorpions. The *desert* of the title, our desert, has no sand in it, but is not merely metaphorical. A harsh, dry place that threatens certain forms of life, it is not a far region we leave home to go out into. On the contrary, we cannot get our of it. Its hot winds blow through our homes, workplaces, schools, and even churches, imbuing them with the climate of the lifeworld we were born into. I do not mean to say that the world is rotten and about to collapse upon its own corruption. The Holy Spirit has not told me that Gabriel is about to blow his horn. I didn't ask.

I mean something very plain. We all live intense, arduous and preoccupied lives. We have so much to do that we pursue even our leisure frantically. When we manage to make a little time for quiet reflection and prayer, we feel the paradoxical need to spend it rather eagerly and "effectively."

Our desert is a desert of busyness.

As one of the means of handling all this, and perhaps of enlivening Sunday worship as well, many serious disciples of Jesus the Lord look for the help of concise reflections that might prompt them into prayer. This book offers that kind of reflection for such men and women, who *hunger and thirst for justice* in this desert of busyness.

Each brief chapter grows out of one Sunday's readings, and falls into three unequal parts. First comes an essay reflecting on what this passage of Scripture and our lifeworld say to each other. The essay does not give a commentary on the readings. Nor does it offer "homily helps" (though many preachers and teachers found the essays in an earlier form useful for that). Instead, each essay proceeds this way: Stand still in the readings of a given Sunday. Look back at the week just past, at relationships and experiences, events and choices; at the intimate and the public, the promising and the threatening. Look forward in the same way to the week coming. That is what these essays try to do. They put the Word and the world in dialog, as the Master did. The essays do this rather boldly, calling on the promise He gave when He said, *"You know the way."*

Second, some statements or questions end each essay. Individuals might find that these suggest further reflection and that they move reflection into prayer. Groups have found that they help focus discussion, though one reality of group process needs to be noted. The group as a whole will succeed much better if each member first speaks out his or her interests or concerns (following the questions or not) before any responds to another. Why? Well, for a reason that does not seem so hard to understand, this helps people to keep coming to the gathering. But at a deeper level, the reason grows from the fact that the Spirit of God illumines each desciple's mind and feeds each heart. We worsen the desert we make pilgrimage through if we do not share with one another what the Spirit gives each of us.

Finally, the end of each essay truns into a prayer. It cannot, of course, take the place of each individuals self-presentation before God. It might make a good summary, though, and since the prayer takes only a minute to read, could function as a weekday reminder of the riches found Sunday in the word of God.

These essays were first written as the column called 'The Word' in *America*, covering the three-year cycle of Sunday readings. I am grateful to the editor, Joseph A. O'Hare, S.J., now president of Fordham University, who invited me to contribute them. The essays as they appear here have been freed of the journalistic compression 'The Word' demanded and in some parts, re-written.

I owe a great deal more than a journalistic opportunity to some others. They are the friends who stand with all of us on the Sundays of many seasons, and invite us to stand with them, listening to the Word and puzzling, even agonizing, over the world. Whether they are *the salt of the earth, the light of the world,* remains a matter of faith. But each of us knows as a matter of fact that they have been salt and light for us, personally. I name some here because their faith and hope have grown to be part of my own and emerge in these pages. Further, I name them to suggest that it is a smart thing for all of us to keep mindful of "the saints" in our lives. In mine, they have been many and faithful: Philip and Margherita DiPasquale of Rhode Island; Joe and Betty Leto of Florida; Bill and Mary Ann Collier, Patricia O'Hara, and Jay Bingle of Connecticut; Bob and Lois Stuber of California; Karl Henion of Texas; and the families Robicheaux, Rousseau, Patron, and Gaudin of Louisiana. Any priest, and man or woman, will be blessed to break bread with such friends through the desert of busyness.

Joseph A. Tetlow, S.J.
Institute of Jesuit Sources
Feast of All Saints, 1987

# 1. Forthright Meddling

*Come back to me with all your heart, fasting, weeping, mourning.*

When the preacher came down hard on gossip, the bristly elder sitting right under the pulpit whispered to himself, "Now that is preaching!" Then the preacher excoriated greed, and promised every kind of decay to those who live off other peoples' sweat. The old man muttered a little louder, "That is true teaching!"

But as he got truly wound up, the preacher arrived at demon rum and intemperance. He had hardly announced the new topic when the old codger said right out loud, "Now he took to meddling!"

It is a feeling any of us might have on Ash Wednesday. The preachers and the readings and the liturgies are going to take to meddling. For all of us know that ashes on the forehead do not call for elegant theologizing. The millennial gesture rather calls for getting practical. It calls, in the old codger's phrase, for forthright meddling. The matters undergoing meddling may seem trivial, but the meddling itself is of some consequence. For the deep theme of every Lent is a saying of Jesus so important that Mark and John carefully stress it and Matthew and Luke report it twice: *"If anyone wants to be a follower of Mine, let him renounce himself, take up his cross and follow Me."*

The problem is this. We can reflect on that saying for years and find no meaning in it unless we are experiencing, in some way, the pressure

1

of death to self. For without the experience of actual renunciation, we will "understand" Jesus' saying about the same way that the angels "understand" human sexual passion. That kind of detached comprehension lays an inadequate basis for deciding and acting in Christ. And yet, in our lifeworld, we are very chary of things that make us *weep and mourn*, and alarmed by things that appear to be psychologically unsound. The human agenda has moved on to self-realization and self-fulfillment. We honestly mean the ashes to signify that we have *come back to God with all our heart;* but we are leery of letting them signify the rest of what Joel prophesied (first reading): *fasting, weeping, mourning.* These activities, we tend to feel therapeutically unsound.

Perhaps one way out of our dilemma is to find ascetical practices that help the integration of our whole person, practices which enact both Good Friday and Easter Sunday, in however small a way.

For instance, we might refuse to molder in front of television and spend time instead with the heroes of great fiction or of Christian history. Or we could give time during the 40 days to gathering a notebook of information needed by any engaged, active citizen. Or how's this for forthright meddling: We might read each week some reflections on the Lenten Sunday's scripture readings. If we get lonesome when we read, we might practice the very current asceticism of going to a meeting of other faithful, or the greater asceticism of gathering such a meeting, weekly.

Now this could be approaching the heroic. For the fact is that many of us consider "sharing the Word" the precise postmodern equivalent of sitting in sackcloth and ashes. Or perhaps boiling supphurous water. Well, we could try another possibility, the opposite of joining a group: in this age of other-directedness, of longing to belong, of living as persons-for-others, we could practice during Lent an asceticism that some of us find hardest of all. We might spend a quarter-hour on it, or half-hour, every day. We heard Jesus say this in the gospel: *"When you pray, go to your private room and, when you have shut your door pray to your Father who is in that secret place, and your Father who sees all that is done in secret will reward you."* Try that daily for 40 days.

These are hardly serious self-denials. But a little desert goes a long way, and we do have to start again somewhere. Otherwise, Jesus' admonition to take up our cross will remain nothing but a metaphor, and a dead letter.

That would be a serious matter.

---

What does it mean that most of us were willing to fast and abstain when all of us were doing it and almost none of us are willing to do it on our own?

What has happened to our grasp of the mystery of sin that we do not any longer appreciate "a mouthful of deadly mushroom" as a metaphor for it?

Can we really have entered an age of "positive asceticism," when we die to our selves by doing instead of by not doing?

---

# Prayer

Lord Jesus Christ,

I accept on my forehead the sign of Your cross,

and into my whole life its reality.

Whatever I find in my living today

that seems inescapable and really hits me hard,

I name with the name of Your cross

and declare that I shoulder it willingly.

Whatever pursues and plagues me

in the tangle of my own mind

and the welter of emotions in my own spirit,

or in the regions of my own lifeworld,

I brand with the sign of Your cross

and beg You, if it be possible,

to let it pass from me, out of my life.

But let all things befall the way You would have them,

and not the way I would have them, merely because I would.

I mark now with the sign of Your cross

all my desiring and yearning,

all my choosing and deciding,

all my enacting and refraining.

And I declare this day:

You are my way, my truth, and my life.

give me, Lord of the Cross, give me to know what I mean.

# 2. Dangers in a Dry Place

*He fasted for 40 days and 40 nights, after which He was very hungry, and the tempter came.*

It has always seemed very odd to hear good Catholics exclaim, for instance after a massive February feast, that they look forward to Lent so they can lose some weight. Some of the feasters mean only to compliment the cuisine, but many betray in the remark a trivializing attitude toward penance. Perhaps that attitude shouldn't seem so odd; after all, the Western Church had domesticated penance and abnegation even before Vatican II. Since the Council, we seem to have reduced penitential practices to that element of silliness that always lurks in them.

The consequences are not happy. For one thing, most of us have no personal experience of the kind of discomfort and suffering that forces us to reassess our life and demands trust in and patience under God— until some grave misfortune or sickness strikes us down. Then, unpracticed at handling this side of the human experience, we let our faith wobble and our hope fade.

Losing the practice of penance, we have lost something precious in the church's tradition, something truly millennial. In fact, we have lost or at least temporarily misplaced an element in Christian life which can be traced right back to Jesus Himself.

Jesus' personal practice of penance emerges most instructively in the story of His temptations in the desert.  For however we understand them—exegetes have worked out several truly illuminating readings—we will find one constant:  Jesus' testing in the desert challenged Him to assess His entire life.  Furthermore, they form the headwaters of a torrent of suffering which washed His life over shoals of rejection and drowned Him in an ocean of pain on the Cross.  In those early trials in the desert, therefore, we can expect to find out a great deal about self-imposed penance, about the kind of basic choices it can lead to, and about its place in our discipleship.

One thing is sure:  we will find out from Jesus' temptations in the desert that fasting is usually the contrary of faddish dieting, the one everything the other is not.  Even medical dieting or dieting just for health's sake do something to help us come to self-concentration and inner calm.  But in a truly penitential person, fasting erodes the vanity and the self-absorption that motivate fad-dieting and all the rest of what Jesus scornfully called *worry about the body.*

Jesus' scorn was not for the body, of course, but for the worry.  To defeat that worry in his own life,  He put Himself into circumstances out in a wild place where He would find worry bootless.  There, *He fasted for 40 days and 40 nights, after which He was very hungry.*  And then *the tempter came,* suggesting that He exercise His powers to make Himself some bread.

Why call this a temptation?  Some exegetes think that Jesus knew already what His claim on the Father included, and how much authority over creation the Father had given Him.  His temptation would then be simply this:  Would He use the power given Him by the Father just for His own comfort?  What kind of man would He be growing into who would demand that the magnificent order of the universe be broached so He could have bread to munch on?

Other exegetes believe the test was subtler than that, though it still touched on material things.  They believe that Jesus was still learning when He went out into the desert what kind of prophet the Lord meant

Him to be, with what kind of powers. His first test, then, embodied this larger choice in a much smaller, symbolical choice: Would He become a Messiah who shook up the social order and re-arranged the distribution of hunger and justice, both? Or would He become a Messiah of a wonderful, utopian Kingdom with plenty of bread?

Well, whatever it meant, He did indeed stay in a desert and He did go hungry. So this much at least is the case, that He did not insist on turning into a Messiah who was the perfect product of human life in His day. He did not grow up to be Galilee's beau ideal, a bronzed splendor who could blur the coldest iris, a totally secure man of position and worth.

Instead, He lived in His whole hungry self the truth that humankind *does not live on bread alone,* on the cycle of harvests and prosperity, on the products of human ingenuity, even on the shared fellowship of tables, alone. His whole self knew that human existence must transcend all of this to live *on every word that comes from the mouth of God.* To be sure that that truth seized Him, He invited into Himself the hollowness of famine and the emptiness of thirst, each of which can be lethal. Where in Him had been human ableness, He consciously put on human helplessness. In doing that, He made flesh His Father's hopes for humankind, which surely transcend the cycle of harvests and, because of sin, go dead against some human hopes.

That is why the followers of Jesus fast, or do any other penance: So that the hopes that the Father entertains for us will not be blanked out in us by a human fulness which is real but passing. Be clear: We do nothing silly by inviting any amount of emptiness in the hope that God Himself will fill the void.

To return to Jesus: The famished emptiness of the Nabatean desert made daydreams and visions likely, and Jesus told His disciples of two others He had. In one of the two, a strange business about leaping off the Temple into the space filled with angels and the cushions of God's tender caring, He faced a complex temptation to demand that God accomplish visible wonders in Him. Some exegetes think that Jesus was being invited to repeat Israel's history of presumption. Some think that Jesus was tempted to force the Father to establish His Sonship with gifts of great renown and unimpeachable status—which of course He would thereupon use for furthering the kingdom. Jesus might well have faced these taunts of the dry Devil.

But His answer here suggests something different from that. He felt Himself invited by His stay in the desert to question why God had led His whole life the way He had indeed led. Was He being tempted to challenge God's wisdom and power, just as Israel had been *that day in at Massah in the wilderness,* when the people had sarcastically wondered why God had led them into a desert to die when there were plenty of graves on the green banks of the Nile? He faced, perhaps, the thought that a boy born of a carpenter and an indescribably beautiful girl might justifiably have anticipated living out his quiet days in his quiet home town. Why would the God of His fathers demand of this Galilean the miserable fate of earlier prophets?

Our own penances can do for us what the desert did for Jesus. They face us with the choice of approving the way the Lord God has led us or of disapproving it. For we cannot choose whatever penances we have a hankering to do; if that is all we do, then we are not doing penance but playing around in the spiritual life. No, the choice of penances facing a mature disciple of Christ is generally dictated by our past. This is particularly true of Christians who have matured in the interior life. We know what has become good for us under God: what leads us to sin; what leads us to greater union with Him; what leads us to greater self-concentration; and what leads us to clearer expressions of love for those He has given us to love. And the more genuine self-denial we practice, the further the Spirit leads us in this knowledge. The disciples knew this before Freud or any contact with Eastern wisdoms. The earliest disciples had learned it from the Master.

Finally, to turn to Jesus one last time. He told His friends that He had seen kingdoms shimmering in a desert haze, luring His allegiance. Exegetes think that perhaps Jesus felt tempted to compromise with evil. In the worst case, some think, He could have felt invited to take an evil means—homage to the Power of Darkness—to reach a good end. In the less-than-worst case, He may have been invited to "be reasonable" and to split the world up with that Power. After all, judgment will come anyhow. And isn't it split up that way right now? We should be able to empathize with this kind of temptation: don't we ourselves feel justified in taking drastic means to save our friends, even if the means are very hard on those who are not our friends? We do not have to be worldweary diplomats to understand how Jesus might have found it attractive to cut a deal with the Devil; we just have to recall the bitter horror humankind has prepared in our nuclear deterrents.

Whatever else the temptation might have meant, Jesus' desert experience brought Him to the point at which He had to say 'yes' to God and 'no' to darkness and to evil.

Any serious and prolonged penance, like a journey through a stretch of desert deep and fierce enough to allow no escape, brings a disciple to the point of choice. Answer yes or no: *You must worship the Lord your God, and serve Him alone.* The penance need not be heroic, just serious and prolonged. In actual practice, the penance will likely appear humiliatingly banal. But banal or draconian, anything will be valuable that brings a person to the point at which he or she can unequivocally make the decision to worship God alone.

Christians have learned the reasonable fear that too fierce penance is just another kind of self-assertion. Destructive, but assertion. We also know that the Master took penance (even fierce penance) seriously. He chose to wrestle with the dangers of dry places. So we do, too. The rest is dieting.

--------------------------------------------------

As always, there is more to think about. What, for instance, did the sinless Jesus find in His own humanness that required "testing" by stretches of desert?

What makes our own commitment to God the Lord so ambiguous as to need proving out?

And then, there is the whole question of keeping a churchly discipline (no meat on Friday, an hour of fasting before Communion) which seems like so many jots and tittles.

---------------------------------------------------

# Prayer

Lord Jesus Christ,
as You grew in wisdom, age, and grace,
You also bent more to the weight of our sin.
You came to sense traces of our foolishness
in words You learned, in images that flooded Your dreams,
in social customs You acted out, even in the priests' teachings.
Yet You embraced the holy disciplines of Your people,
their attempt to flee their structured sin.

Walking dangerous dry places filled with demons,
forty days hungry and burning with noonday thirst,
You emptied Yourself utterly and stood before God.

Lord, we have grown in wisdom and age and grace
among a people who blur the lines
between the sacred and the secular,
and we wander from day to day to day
in a desert of busyness
hungry for God's love, thirsty for His holiness.

Steady us still through the dangers of this dry place.

# 3. The Desert of Busyness

*The Spirit drove Him out into the wilderness.*

Macarius the Egyptian, a great desert father, led the monks of the desert in opposing the Arian heresy. His zeal proved more intense than his bishop's, unhappily, and he eventually provoked the bishop not only to censure him, but to punish him by separating him from his monk-friends. In fact, Macarius was forced to leave his beloved desert and move to a lush, fruitful island in the middle of the Nile. His island of exile was the kind of place lined with posh resorts today, and most of the rest of us would have been tempted sorely to provoke an extended sentence. Not Macarius. As soon as he could, he escaped and fled back to his desert in the West. He feared and despised what he felt a too ready accommodation by Christians to a newly friendly world, in which martyrdom was no longer standard government operating procedure. He jettisoned the sensuous sophistication of fourth-century Egypt, preferring to battle acedia, the noonday devil, and to feel his spirit change and grow in God's love under the disciplines of solitude, hunger, thirst, and scorching heat.

Macarius felt driven into the desert by the Spirit of God, as surely as his Master had and as surely as the whole People of God had, through that same Egyptian desert and into the Sinai.

In that desert, the Spirit teaches us that God is the author of life; we are not. There, the Spirit fires into His vessels of clay hope in God's

**11**

faithfulness to His own word: *I establish My covenant with you; nothing of flesh shall be swept away again* (first reading), not by *the waters of the flood* and not by the dry enmity of the desert. Here is the strange reversal worked by every desert. The place seems empty, a long latitude of sameness, sounding—if it sounds anything at all—only a hot, soporific hum. But this dead waste teems with life, because here the Spirit of God "broods over the bent world," and here particularly this Spirit shows how to turn again to life.

If deserts are that good, shouldn't we look for one? Shouldn't any serious disciple who wants to find God more surely be searching for some kind of desert? The fact is that a lot of us are looking—into TM, food disciplines, week-long seminars on self-appropriation, and into the silence of directed retreats.

But a further fact is that, given the lifestyles open to us at this time, we actually do not have to go searching at all. If we listen to the Spirit, we are not likely to feel compelled to squint our way into the baking rincon of the monastery of Christ in the Desert at Abiquiú, New Mexico. We are more likely to find the Spirit teaching us that our deserts have already grown into our everyday lives, the way Africa's are spilling sand further and further south into once fertile valleys.

What are our deserts?

Busyness is the main one and certainly the most all embracing. This busyness does not refer to the compulsive activity we name "workaholism," since workaholism rises from within a person and not from his or her environment. Workaholism is not a desert, it is an emotional and/or a spiritual problem. The busyness addressed here rises from our virtues—from personal gifts and skills, from Christlike commitment and concern, from trying to live as a person-for-others. Precisely because of our virtues, almost every one of us finds it necessary to be relentlessly on the go. We live tightly constrained by clocks, commuting and commitments. We feel that we "haven't got time," the way a pilgrim in a desert hasn't got cool shade. We find the press of affairs around us setting our agenda for us, just the way the harsh requirements of desert life set the agenda there. We can easily find a phone call from a friend a thorn in the day; and meetings, as empty and dry as the Dead Sea's shore.

Our busyness can stretch out before us as unending as Death Valley and just as desolate, keeping us hungry and thirsty and without repose. It can threaten our interior life, just as the Egyptian desert threatened Macarius's physical life. Macarius fought listlessness and tedium in his desert, the noonday devil; in our desert of busyness, we fight frenzy and exhaustion, a kind of darknight devil.

The parents of little children will find rearing their children a true desert, and one into which they go for the same reason Jesus went into His desert: to find love. An executive secretary needs no instruction about deserts, considering how completely he or she must structure personal feelings, desires, and even needs to the busyness of the day and even of the moment. Police officers, bank tellers, construction workers, every kind of commuter—all of us are tested by busyness and each of us can come to know ourselves very clearly through this testing. Whether we have a desert or not is not the issue. The only real issues are the issues that faced Jesus when He went into His desert: Whom only do I serve first and before all? Where is my real source of life? What do I hope for beyond and outside of this dry, hot busyness?

Busyness is not our only desert; we walk through others. Noise makes one, for instance. Going from day to day, few of us can escape inane stretches of din and racket. The interior of our homes are sandblasted by television's spray-can laughter, and most public places rattle with radio's punishing decibels. Even when we find our way into the Grand Tetons or out onto the Appalachian Trail, we are likely to be pursued by someone's tinny transistor boring into our cringing ear. Through all these noises, our spirits are deliberately and cunningly excited by tastemakers. Macarius, blown weary by the hot sirocco, fought apathy and boredom in his desert; in ours, we fight agitation and anxiety, afflicted by a steady and strident cacaphony. But we fight just as truly as Macarius ever did.

Mature Christians easily identify other deserts:  a painful illness;  a stretch of prescribed drug-taking (particularly mood-altering drugs); a tense, unhappy work-situation that can not now be escaped; a trying passage in a child's growing up.  These are true deserts, which we cannot wave away with a magic wand—and in which our lifeworld tries our spirit severely.

If we willingly and patiently traverse these deserts, the Spirit willingly gives us to know God as the Source of our life, there plainly in those locales being no other.  The Spirit will further teach us to trust God, leading us to the quiet and stillness of self-abandonment.  Some day soon, on a day the Father has already set, the Spirit of Life will hover over this chaos we make for ourselves and in irresistible power enliven it with living water and calm it with gracious green peace.  But until then, we can very reasonably take busyness and noise and illness and every kind of trying passage as deserts.

Our task when we get a taste of one of these deserts is to live such steady and calm lives as to give evidence of some secret, Whom we will name if asked.

-----------------------------------------------------------

There is more to ponder about these deserts.  The too-brief list of current deserts, for instance, could be extended by deserts each of us lives through.

We of the First World have to wonder how it is that the more we consume, the worse our desert of busyness grows.

And then we could draw up Laws for Surviving Whatever Desert.

-----------------------------------------------------------

# Prayer

Spirit Of The Living God,
You drove the Lord Jesus
into a desert dry with death,

empty of everything living but Your own presence,
and there You taught Him hope
and the quiet possession of His own self.

Lord who breathes life into all that lives,
You have chosen the time and place of our lives.

You have summoned us to a lifeworld
seared with winds of confusion and dissention,
teeming with desperate needs,
scorched with avarice and anxieties
and cowed under the fear of an apocalyptic end.

Gentle Lord, breathe freshly on us;
as You defended Jesus from illusion and despair,
so defend us, and teach us
the quiet possession of our own selves.

# 4. The Forty Days

*Having exhausted all these ways of tempting Him, the devil left Him, to return at the appointed time.*

For 40 days and 40 nights, Moses fasted, then brought down from Mt. Horeb the commandments of the Covenant. For 40 years the People of God wandered in the desert, then came to the Promised Land. Jesus' 40 days in the desert recapitulate all that, whether Luke's incident was truly a single one or is rather a conflation of several, the way Matthew's Sermon on the Mount seems to be. As a consequence, His temptations are luminously symbolic.

But we have to be careful not to let them turn into mere symbols. Jesus is flesh and blood and His testing was real, *for we do not have a high priest who is unable to sympathize with our weakness, but one who was tempted in every way that we are.* The church recalls His temptations as Lent begins because they remind us of a crucial truth about our own real testing.

For we can hardly expect to grasp how we have sinned if we do not grasp how we have been tempted. And in our day, we have trivialized temptation and think of it in merely moral terms, as an impulse to break a law or to go against the dictates of our own consciences. We too rarely reflect that, for God's chosen, beneath each moral temptation is a religious test.

16

Thus, in the Old Testament, "temptation" always means that a partner in the Covenant is being tested. Will He be faithful? Will they be loyal? Will He or they fulfill the conditions agreed to and deliver what was promised? Nowhere in the Old Testament are pagans and unbelievers said to be tempted197only the Chosen. The Lord tests His people and in their turn, the people test their God. Psalm 78 puts it poignantly: *Again and again they tempted God.*

Within this history of His people, Jesus comes to bring the Covenant to fulfillment. He must determine what kind of Messiah He will be, for His people have varying expectations. Will He give them what they want: everlasting manna, political dominion, a king to take their responsibilities for them? Or will He lead them to feel the pain of outranged conscience, to bear in patience the consequences of humankind's sin, and even to embrace death willingly, as the ultimate earthly punishment for our willful rebellion? Jesus faced such decisions, and His choices reveal the more public meaning of His temptations in the desert.

About making bread of desert stones, for instance: Yahweh had promised to provide food for His people and had kept His promise by giving them manna in the desert. But they failed on their side, craving fleshpots, railing in discontent, then in doubt, then in disbelief.

Citizens of a consumer society have no trouble understanding what the people went through, since our own society is structured to keep us from ever being content with what we have. It must, if we are to keep consuming. Unhappily, that discontent seeps into our interior lives, erupting in more noxious desires than a hankering for the newest software and not bottoming out in a lust for the latest in jeans. Late in the game, unless we have grown reflective, our discontent stretches to the way God is furnishing our lifeworld. Unhappy with our brand of manna, we stew in discontent and doubt and then we find it easy to disbelieve that God cares very much. We figure we just need better "breaks" or we just have to work harder to improve the quality of our lives. What has God to do with that passing stuff?

Those who find problems taking all this in need only examine what they mean when they ask God, *Give us this day our daily bread.* Just bread? If not, then what else? And how much else?

In Jesus' second temptation (as Luke lists them) about the kingdoms, the issue is not whether God's kingdom will overcome, but to whom Jesus will owe His victory. Shall there be homage done, and to whom?

The past taught Jesus a lesson. For the Israelites—the story is told in the passage in Deuteronomy from which Jesus takes His response to Satan—had come into the Promised Land and, although they had been warned against the danger, promptly *forgot God.* This is the religious temptation. Any human can live out law and conscience and become very good and beautiful, but Christians have made a covenant to do more: *You shall do homage to the Lord your God.* Perhaps one of our temptations is precisely to serve what we think of as our consciences instead of our God. Perhaps our failure is thus to do homage to technological humanity or to secular humanism, and to put our trust there. What kindgom do we really mean: *Thy kingdom come?* Do we envision a true kingdom, or an egalitarian utopia?

With Jesus' third temptation, to test God in direct action by leaping into danger, we come back to moral questions, but at a deep level. The question involves consciously violating law and conscience. When those who are baptized in Christ do this in grave matters, they take a terrifying risk similar to throwing themselves off the temple and requiring God to save them. For Christian moral practices grow out from Christian belief and then in turn protect that belief from the abrasions of daily life, a little bit the way the tortoise's shell grows out of its fleshy life and then becomes its home. Christians who live within their conscience's dictates live safely at home. Christians who persist in serious sin tear away the defenses of their belief and dare God to keep it alive nonetheless.

The deterioration shows up in established patterns. When we violate our own consciences, we unleash a virulent disorder into our own lives. If we violate them (actually, violate our selves) much, we live in confusion and our interior lives grow dark and ugly. Anyone living like that will soon find it too difficult to believe in a God who *orders all things sweetly from end to end.* It proves easier not to believe. And that is how many fail the morals test.

But what if we pass these tests, as Jesus passed them? Suppose we live grateful to God, and eagerly worship Him, and trust that His Spirit speaks through our conscience's voice?

Well, we can no more expect to be let alone than Jesus was. There are further tests of our belief in God and our hope in Him. The spirit of darkness will *return at the appointed time.*

------------------------------------------------------

So, there are further things to think about. Can't every one of us name things that have tested us beyond ordinary moral matters, and right down to our faith commitment?

What do we refer to when we ask God, *lead us not into temptation?*

How can we fit together *being tested* and *taking up the cross daily?*

------------------------------------------------------

# Prayer

Lord Jesus Christ,
even though You kept Your own conscience clear,
You never felt self-righteous or self-justified.

Instead, You gave Yourself to the guidance of the Holy Spirit
and at times against what we think common sense
You chose step by step to serve God and Him only.

Lord, You have tasted all that we taste, even our confusion.
We consume great quantities of earth's goods,
and are solicited every day to go and get more of them.

We hear every day of decisions that shake our world
and we are driven to wonder whether the Father watches.

We feel confused every day by our own prophets and teachers
and sometimes do not know, Whom shall we follow?

Lord Jesus, tested and proven good,
You know how to steady us in our choices
to find God and to serve God first and in everything.

We choose now to follow You.

# 5. Shot Through with Sublime Glory

*When they raised their eyes, they saw no one but only Jesus.*

The event on the Mount of Transfiguration stunned Peter, James, and John. They saw with their own eyes how splendid God intends our bones to be, *for His own purpose and by His own grace in Christ Jesus* (second reading). But the event was an event, not the whole history. When it was past, even the three who had witnessed Jesus shot through with *Sublime Glory* still had a lot of believing to do.

They and the other disciples had gotten a solid start on believing, long before going up that mountain. Early on, they had grown into the conviction that Jesus was indeed *the One to come.* They had watched the blind begin to see and the lame start to walk. They had stood among the poor as Good News was proclaimed to them. So, long before the Master took them up the mountain, the three had grown convinced that the People of God did not have to wait for someone else. The Promised One had indeed come.

Not everyone around shared their faith. Not long before they went up the Mount of Transfiguration and not very far away from it, Peter had watched appalled as the crowd melted away from the One he had come to believe in. And then he had led an elite among Jesus' disciples to a deeper faith. There at Caesarea Philippi, Peter had poured out his belief that Jesus had an altogether extraordinary relationship with the Father. *"You are the Christ, the Son of the living God."* Then the others said the same thing.

What did Peter and the rest mean by *the Son of the living God*? In the beginning, no doubt, they meant what the Law and the Prophets had taught them: The Chosen One was to be a unique person, anointed by the Spirit of God, who would in his own self embody and represent the whole People of God. That tradition had begun with Abraham, whose *only child Isaac, whom you love [your Beloved One]*, personified in his own little body the innumerable people God meant to draw from Abraham's seed. Seeing Isaac, Abraham saw the realization of God's promise to make him the father of multitudes.

The first of those "multitudes" was Israel. They arrived in the promised land a fairly ragged band, but they multiplied and covered the land. As the centuries went by, this multitude came to be thought of as one representative person. So Moses could hurl this into Pharaoh's face: *"This is what Yahweh says: 'Israel is my first-born son.'"* The whole people was personified, made the child of God the Father. Then the centuries wore on, and this personification of the whole people again came to be identified with a single, real person. Psalm 2, for instance, has Yahweh declare to a king whom He has enthroned *in Zion, my holy mountain: "You are my son, today I have become your father."* Later still, Isaiah described this person who embodied the whole people in himself. He would be kingly in unique ways, and the Lord God would declare of him: *"Here is my Servant whom I uphold, My Chosen One in whom My soul delights."*

Even when the Word was made flesh, the full meaning of this anointed person's relationship with the Father had not yet broken clear. So when they went with Jesus up the mountain, Peter, James, and John could not yet have committed themselves to the most stunning sense in which Jesus is God's Son. Perhaps unavoidably, Peter and the brothers Boanerges had to spend all His lifetime coming to see what John the Evangelist would be able to put bluntly only two generations after Jesus'

Resurrection: *"I and the Father are one."* During His lifetime, after all, they not only walked with Him and went fishing with Him—they also argued with Him. They needed considerable distance from all that before they could fully comprehend why the Sanhedrin would cry *"Blasphemy!"* and plan his execution instead of expostulating crossly, "Oh, Faugh!" and tossing Him in jail.

So when the three went up the Mount of Transfiguration, they recognized Him as the Promised One, the embodiment of the whole people. It made perfect sense to them that Moses the Lawgiver should show up, whose face had shone after talking with God; and that Elijah the prophet of prophets would come, who had been assumed into heaven at his life's end. But what overwhelmed them was nothing human. What turned their minds to liquid mirrors was the real Presence, the Shekinah: the Most Holy One. God the Lord suddenly seized them in their lifeworld the way a sheet of lightning sheers attention from everything else around, leaving faces white. In their whole being, the three knew God's intent: *"This is My Son, the Beloved."*

In the end, *when they raised their eyes, they saw no one but only Jesus* (Gospel).

Of course. He now sums up in His own person the whole of the Law and the Prophets. He Himself is now the *covenant of the people and the light of nations.* In the man Jesus now rests the whole of God's power, the whole of His ineluctable promise. Then it rests in the humanity He has taken to Himself and filled with grace. Incredulously, fearfully, His disciples came to understand that His Transfiguration prefigures our own: *Indeed, from His fulness we have, all of us, received—yes, grace in returnfor grace.* We may not catch many glints of *sublime glory,* but all of us together are made over in His transfigured likeness.

Some exegetes now wonder whether the Transfiguration actually took place just as it is described in the Gospels. That's no surprise: A human corruscating with divine holiness does rather stretch the mind, in any generation. And anyhow, it would appear that disciples wondered about it early on. So the third and fourth generation of disciples, as though in answer to the doubt whether the Tranfiguration had indeed taken place, found it useful to remember something Peter had liked to say (it is in 2 Peter):

*It was not any cleverly invented myths that we were repeating when we brought you the knowledge and power and the coming of our Lord Jesus Christ: We had seen His majesty for ourselves. He was honored and glorified by God the Father, when the Sublime Glory itself spoke to Him and said, "This is My Son, the Beloved: He enjoys My favor."*

The thing is, Peter and the others kept insisting that each man and woman who accepts Jesus Christ as Lord also enjoys the Father's favor. This is the root problem with the Transfiguration today, and perhaps from the beginning it has been the problem. For the final implications of the Transfiguration are utterly incredible. We are all of us—all of the baptized into Christ Jesus—shot through with the *Sublime Glory.*

The earliest disciples came first to believe that Jesus was the One to Come, the One who embodied the People and went on ahead to represent them before the Throne. But they had to work hard to believe that the Christ is equal to God the Father. Perhaps we give ourselves trouble by turning that around. Perhaps we come to assert too easily that Jesus Christ is God, truly one with the Father. We can hold Him, that way, rather at a distance. But we do not as easily believe that He is the Covenant made personal in our flesh, and that *by His blood* we are all made one in our humanity, all children of God, co-heirs of the Firstborn, but only together.

Since we do not dwell yet wholly transfigured by the *Sublime Glory,* we need a lot of faith to acknowledge that.

---------------------------------------------------------

So there remains much to ponder. For instance, the crowd in church last Sunday who couldn't even sing. They are the ones around whom we are to see a nimbus of divinity?

Well, we can at least name real living men and women whose selves are transformed in Christ.

And any of us can rightly claim that we have been transformed--even transfigured—when at privileged times in our life the *Sublime Glory* has seized us.

--------------------------------------------------

# Prayer

Lord, mighty God,
your Holy Presence lights universes beyond our reach
and illumines with the intimate glow of life
each secret part of our body.

As you seized Jesus of Nazareth
and filled Him with *Sublime Glory,*
the life that is the source of life,
so you have seized us through His Spirit,
and chosen to gaze upon us with favor,
and marked us with His Name,
and assigned us a privileged role in Your Reign,
and made us a source of life
for all whom you put in our lifeworld.

Here in this moment,
even without being able to see the splendor
of those made lightsome with your Presence,
we choose to gaze with favor on all around us,
as you gaze on us.

# 6. Delivered Up to High Places

*God did not spare His own Son, but gave Him up to benefit us all.*

Abraham and Sarah had yearned for offspring year after fruitless year until their time had passed. So when it was revealed to them that they would conceive a son, they giggled in their incredulity. They were still laughing when old Sarah bore him: They named him Isaac, which means "he laughs."

Some babies really do laugh, but the glee in this case seems to have died fast. When Isaac was still a little boy, Abraham's faith in Yahweh came to a time of severe trial. History has not told us why. Had he been derelict in offering sacrifices to El Shaddai? Anyone who refuses to enact his faith by worship finds it shrinking down to an appendix in the gut of life, and his problems with it can become acute. Whatever the antecedents, Abraham trailed up a stubbled desert promontory, a three-day walk from his home, followed by his splendid child. His spirit felt like desert scoured by sandpaper wind. His mind was set on offering to God *his son, his only son* (first reading). For he had grown convinced that fidelity to God demanded that of him just now.

Was the whole hot scene just a hideous dream that kept old Abraham thrashing through a sick night? Or did he actually climb up a "high

26

land" to spill his own son's blood? We do not think we know right now, really. But we do know that the People of God saw a model in Abraham anyhow, and the earliest Christians saw two models.

First, through the centuries, the people saw in Abraham the model of the believer, the person who put such utter trust in God as to give the same quick response even to the most excruciating of demands, *"Here I am."* They saw his faith rewarded with the most amazing blessing ever given a man, *and one already as good as dead himself: more descendants than could be counted,* as the author of Hebrews put it. Abraham's faith founded a whole people and the world's redemption.

The people's devotion to Abraham passed on to the disciples of Jesus, and the early Christians also took Abraham as a model of faith. They saw something else, too. They saw in his willingness to sacrifice his son a model of the willingness of the Father to give over His Son. Paul alludes to this when he says to the Romans, *God did not spare His own Son, but gave Him up to benefit us all* (second reading).

Four points emerge from the parallel between God the Father and Abraham.

First: Abraham loved his son, and the Father loved His Son, and their loves never faltered. We know this theoretically, but when we suffer the least bit, we tend to think like Isaac when the wood bit into his knees and shins. Could this man really love him?

He did. But—this is the second point—if Abraham really walked up that hill, then he was driven to desperation by some dark madness. We must be extremely alert not to allege such a dark madness or any desperation in God. We may be at a loss to explain why Jesus suffered and died; we may not recoup that loss by alleging that the Father loved the Son so incompletely as to wish Him any harm whatever, let alone mortal harm. *"I and the Father are one,"* Jesus said, and *"everything the Father has is mine,"* beginning with life.

Hence, third, Jesus the man trusted His father as utterly as young Isaac had trusted his. The boy had wondered, loaded with wood for the sacrifice and trailing his father who had *in his own hands the fire and the knife,* where the victim might be. *"My son, God Himself will provide the lamb"* is all his father would say; *then the two of them went on together.*

Early Christians made much of God providing the Lamb, and we still do. But what we need to note today is the trust—Isaac's complete trust in Abraham and Jesus' complete trust in the Father. We may find it impossible to imagine Jesus' passion and death precisely because we are unable to imagine a trust in God so penetrating that it can say, *"Nevertheless, let Your will be done, not mine,"* even under the shadow of the cross.

Jesus is the victim of the cross. But if there is talk of a victim between Abraham and Isaac, there is no such talk between Jesus and the Father. Abraham meant to offer the boy to Yahweh. Jesus is truly the Lamb, the victim, but theologians feel repelled at the thought of the Father offering His Son to Himself.

Then in what sense did *God not spare His own Son, but give Him up to benefit us all?*

Here is the fourth point. Among many possible meditations about the meaning of *God not sparing His own Son,* this thought stands out now: The Father sent the Son into humankind as it stood steeped in sin. The Son was indeed to enter wholly into humanity, even into the deepest recesses of humanity, where unconsciousness is a granitic weight, where hideous resentments run into molten anger, where love and hate overlap in violence. The Son did not skim the surface of our real being; He plunged in like a nun into a wardroom full of unattended plague victims. He embraced a humanity that tears at itself like the possessed, and he flung Himself into that confict with all of its accompanying confusion. His human life, in the end, was destroyed by the viciousness in our humanity.

But His life—as none ever before—was destroyed only ineffectually, for God had dreamed of a way to give His only Son even more totally than to the point of death, because *He loved the world so much.* He gave the Son not only to die, but also to rise. So the Father's "giving over" matched the Son's "raising up": Both had two moments, one of death and one of life.

Another incident on another mountain, without parallel in Abraham's life: the Transfiguration. This time, the Son trailed up the stubbled track, followed not by offspring but by friends through whom He would beget a new people. His agenda, remembered by Luke, was union in that high place with His Father, and discourse with the great of His people's past, Moses and Elijah, about *his passing (his exodus* is the word used by the Gospel), *which He was to accomplish in Jerusalem.* That communion worked a change in Him; He gave His consent to the Father's hopes, and became incandescent in the thought of what His Father proposed to do.

As Paul would later write to the Romans, *He not only died for us—He rose from the dead for us, and went up to the highest place of all, where at God's right hand He stands and pleads for us.*

We cannot, therefore, comprehend how the Father "delivered Him up" unless we remember this outcome in glory. Even so, during a privileged time of the Church's year, we make sure not to trivialize the glory, by pondering faithfully the cost of it.

-------------------------------------------------------

All this suggests a lot to think about, beginning here: To what has the Father of our Lord Jesus Christ *delivered us up?*

In our lifeworld, where religiously dramatic actions are inherently suspect because of the "witness" of insane leaders of sects and inane preachers in the electronic media, we have to ask what dramatic actions are available to us for expressing total fidelity to God? And who today models those dramatic actions for us?

How does Jesus' rising from the dead complete the way the Father gave His own Son to humankind?

-------------------------------------------------------

# Prayer

Faithful God, Father of our Lord Jesus Christ, You sent Your own Son
into everything desperate and dark in our humanity,
while we were still sunk in our sinfulness,
never demanding that we make ourselves sinless and sane
before You would further show your love for us
and send Him among us in our flesh.

Teach us to find Him where He hides—
still in our humanity, still in our flesh,
always working to heal and save where there is pain,
always pouring out His Spirit of Life
even where we sin and deal death to ourselves.

As You saved Him out of the jaws of death,
save us, and bring us and many with us
into His reign of life.

# 7. The Pattern of His Death

*We are waiting for the Lord Jesus Christ, and He will transfigure these wretched bodies of ours into copies of His glorious body. He will do that by the same power with which He can subdue the whole universe.*

His Transfiguration surely proved one of the more extraordinary things Jesus did or had happen to Him. It was unusual even in not being much talked about during His lifetime, although just about everything else was, including things He wanted kept quiet. Since the Transfiguration suggests several things to His disciples about suffering and glory, we need to let the event instruct us.

The incident begins this way in Luke's narrative: Jesus *took Peter, James, and John and went onto a mountain to pray.* Jesus regularly went off by Himself to pray, and He habitually prayed before any important action. For instance, before choosing the Twelve, *He went out to the mountain to pray, spending the night in communion with God.* He taught the Our Father one day *when He had finished praying in a certain place.* In fact, in every locale where He did extended public ministry, Jesus picked out *a certain place* where he could spend time by Himself in quiet. So, for example, all of His friends, including Judas, knew where He would disappear to after Passover supper. He would be across Kedron in Gethsemani, praying.

Well, those of us who feel the need to go off to some *certain place* where we can pray in quiet, should recognize Whom we are like in this.

We need not make too much of it; having a sort of holy spot for ourselves has not so far shown up as a cause for canonization. Neither ought we make too little of it; after all, it was the Master who gave us the example of finding our own little oasis in this desert of busyness. We do well to be like Him in this.

We might be like Him in another way if we sometimes tell friends about our own prayer, and listen to them talk about theirs. For Jesus was not exactly reticent about His prayer. Once, for instance, He told His disciples about a vision He had had in which He saw Satan fall from heaven like lightning. And it must have been Jesus Himself who told about the angels of comfort in Gethsemani; the three who were with Him there seem to have slept soundly through it all. Hence, Jesus let His friends know something about His union with God in prayer, and even about His visions.

He was surely doing that when he took three of His closest friends and went up the Mount of Transfiguration.

There, Luke reports, Jesus, Moses, and Elijah *spoke of His passage which He was about to fulfill in Jerusalem.* Jesus had made sure that His three closest companions would hear this conversation. These three knew perfectly well what the glorious saints meant by *His passage,* since they were talking just after Jesus had predicted for the first time that He would go up to Jerusalem and die. As He had in other circumstances, Jesus told the three on the way down the mountain that they were to tell no one about the conversation until after the Son of Man had finished suffering and risen again.

It seems as though He need not have worried. Peter, James, and John do not appear to have been eager to think about Jesus' coming suffering, let alone share with others the tremendous consolation they received through Jesus while hearing about *His exodus.* They were completely baffled that in the middle of all this glory and power, the talk should be about suffering.

We should have no trouble understanding their bafflement. For in the midst of all the glory and power of our lifeworld's technological achievements and our nation's bountiful resources, we do not much like to think about suffering, either. In particular, perhaps because we see worlds of human suffering nightly in living color, we have become disinclined to remember and pray over Jesus' suffering. Very many of us, for instance, recently read in a leaflet placed in the pews the reasons why we observe Lent. We found as the first reason the preparation to celebrate Christ's Resurrection. We found several others, including some sage objectives in self-discipline and penitence. We did not find listed as one main reason for observing Lent the remembrance of Christ's Passion and Death.

Whatever the reasons, we disciples today are not like the earliest disciples when it comes to remembering the Lord's passion. They wrote down the narrative of that passion before they wrote down anything else, as though of all things they wanted most to preserve that story. Even as they rollicked through the first days of the Spirit's season, right in the midst of all the tongues of fire and the glossolalia and the conversions and the miracles, they remembered His passion. So a little later, Paul would remind the Corinthians that *every time you eat this bread and drink this cup, you are proclaiming his death.*

That came later, after the Resurrection. When they walked down the Mount of the Transfiguration, Peter, James, and John seem not to have passed on Jesus' example of pondering the pains of human existence while in the Presence. We know that Jesus instructed them not to, but we also know that they went right ahead and talked about everything else He instructed them not to talk about. So we do not really know why the three did not help the others ponder Jesus' coming trial. One thing we do know: if they were unable to ponder or even envision Jesus suffering before His Resurrection, they were more than able to keep it in mind after it. Perhaps they needed to experience the power at work in themselves before they could face suffering.

We are like them in that. For it may well be that, as digital thinking in bits and bites takes hold of our consciousness, we think of Jesus' Passion and of our own sins which contribute to it in separate compartments. We may not have grasped *His passage* as a whole, which means

His death and His rising, His going down and His coming back up. When Luke called the Transfiguration *His exodus,* the literary-minded evangelist certainly intended the metaphorical comparison with the exodus of the People of God from bondage, for Jesus' Transfiguration presages His going out of a life on this earth which had to end in death into a life in God's glory which will never end.

So we learn this from the three who went up the Mount: Those who do not truly believe in and earnestly look forward to their own resurrection—a belief and hope accepted through steady prayer—will not easily accompany Jesus through His Passion. They will not ponder it and they will never imitate it. They will not understand at all why Christians avoid many things as evil and destructive which much of the rest of humankind think harmless fun and games, and why we embrace as lifegiving and creative some things that many others flee. In brief, they do not understand that we must go down into the depths of humanity with Jesus Christ in order to rise again with Him made new.

Those of us who have experienced God's power at work in us and live actively hoping for our own resurrection are able to accompany Jesus through His sufferings. We can understand what Paul meant when he wrote to the Philippians: *All I want is to know Christ and the power of His resurrection and to share His sufferings by reproducing the pattern of His death. That is the way I can hope to take my place in the resurrection of the dead.*

Up on the Mount of Transfiguration, the disciples learned about *reproducing the pattern of His death.* They knew from the start that it did not necessarily mean having implacable and murderous enemies and dying affixed to a cross. They did rejoice, though, when their lifeworld dealt with them just the way it had dealt with the Master. But the *pattern of His death* fits everyone's lifeworld, murderous enemies or no.

Here are some of the things that it means: Jesus allowed the Power of God to seize Him, and to give the basic shape to His life, even when He began to perceive mortal danger. He accomplished that by prayer, even by scouting out the places where He could pray and by going regularly to them. In His prayer, in the Presence, He pondered human suffering and then the stark realities He faced. He did that before God, and not apart from God. He did not keep these experiences in the Presence to Himself, but shared them with His friends. More than that, He let His friends' experiences of prayer touch Him, as when He found Himself confirmed and filled with joy by His disciples' profession of faith in Him.

We have already in us, as Peter, James, and John had in them, the power to *reproduce the pattern of His death.* We have that power whether we have mortal enemies or not, and whether we find ourselves called on to suffer greatly or to enjoy expansively. For through the Holy Spirit, God the creator has begun to accomplish the promise: *He will give a new form to this lowly body of ours and remake it according to the pattern of His glorified body* (second reading). We recall that vividly when we recall the Transfiguration. We need to keep it vividly in mind so that we can accompany Him through His sufferings, and so that our own "exodus" will take on its full meaning.

For the full lesson that His disciples learned reaches to this: that we are so far united to Jesus Christ that the sufferings we undergo in our own bodies *make up all that has still to be undergone by Christ for the sake of his body, the Church.*

-----------------------------------------------------

So the Transfiguration suggests some things to think about, the first of which is whether we find it good to have special places to pray.

Then, we could ponder what keeps us from praying as the earliest disciples prayed, attentive to the price He paid for our salvation.

There remains a bottom line: How does our *exodus* differ from just going through life and exiting it?

-----------------------------------------------------

# Prayer

Lord Jesus Christ,
You grew up listening to long and wordfilled prayer,
going with the people to synagogue to pray.

When Your time came, though You loved the house of God,
You also found Your own places.

You prayed more and more as danger tightened around You,
and shared with friends more and more
of what You found in the Presence.

Master of our prayer, hand on to us what You learned,
how we have been made temples of the Spirit,
and how in our own hearts, according to their own beating,
we are able to make all the prayer the Father means in us.

We ask You this who in the desert of busyness,Rout of a lifeworld
thrashing under cruel tyrannies,
lifted Your own mind and Your own heart
and held Your attention before the Throne of God
praying in the day and in the night,Rin Your own special places,
even in a garden ripened with agony.

# 8. Very Reliable Source

*"The water that I shall give will turn into a spring inside him, welling up to eternal life."*

Although two-thirds of the earth is covered with water, more than half of all humankind do not have ready access to sweet, pure water. Worse than that, many have to drink water that quenches their life as it quenches their thirst; of people who die from disease, eight out of ten die from diseases transmitted by the water they use. So when more than half of all people living today drink a cup of water, they can be drinking their deaths.

The other half, the affluent, expect clear, safe water to pour from every faucet the way we expect the sun to rise. We consider universally available potable water almost a birthright, and certainly a well established achievement of American technology and social engineering. We feel no great ambiguity about water, and if we have let it settle as a symbol in our imaginations, it is as a blue puddle in the back yard, full of sunshine and chlorine, concretizing upscale leisure.

We are the exception in human history. Most peoples have had to fight for good water, and most peole felt very ambiguous about rain and rivers and oceans. The entire ancient world considered water the site of and common accompaniment to divine epiphanies and at the same times also the abode of and the vehicle for demonic powers. This ambiguity—waters as both blessing and fearsome threat—shapes many passages in both the Old and the New Testament. It instructs us when we ponder the truth that *the love of God has been poured out into our hearts by the Holy Spirit which has been given us* (second reading), making us a source of life for ourselves and for others as well.

Here is what Jesus wanted us to understand. Every one of us has to watch that we are reliable sources of life, *welling up to eternal life,* for the others that God puts into our lives. Far from being noxious sources, welling up to poison the lives of those around us, we disciples ought not even prove ambiguous sources welling up to the more temporary versions of life so ready to our hands.

The Old Testament, to begin at the beginning, depicts water as a mighty force. Genesis begins depicting God *moving over the face of the deep,* driving back the chaos of waters and drawing order from them. But the waters remain inimical to humankind, and spill out again in the flood (the Hebrew word for which means "cataclysm"). God the Lord continues the struggle against the waters: The psalmist sings: " *The waters saw that it was you, God...they recoiled...shuddered to their depths,* as an enemy might. Even *if the waves of death encircled* me," the psalmist goes on, as though telling about a war, "God the Lord *defeats them and draws me from deep waters."*

For all that, the People of God knew springs and rivers as life-giving. The most life-giving of all was the great four-branched, abundant river that really made Paradise. Dwellers in a dry land, they considered sweet water altogether precious, and a beautiful sign of God's blessings. They never forgot that the Red Sea had let them pass and then trapped their enemies, and they remembered the sweet waters in the desert at Meribah: Moses *struck the rock...waters gushed, torrents streamed out* (first reading). Then Jordan had spontaneously run dry so that they could enter into the land of this promise: *And you will draw water joyfully from the springs of salvation.*

Among the ancients, then, water meant death and water meant life, and their ambiguity toward it runs deeper than can easily be summarized. The Hebrew words for "spring," for instance, etymologically mean much the same as the word for "eye": The ancients once regarded springs as mother earth weeping! That's what they had to drink so that's what they drank.

Even in the less ancient times of the New Testament, water kept its ambiguous meanings. The Gerasene pigs, for instance, leapt into depths of the sea as if that were the natural element of the demons who had possessed them. And a demon threw the possessed lad not only into fire, but also into water in order to injure him. The Sea of Galilee stormed up to destroy Jesus and the disciples, but Jesus "rebuked" it— just the way Yahweh had rebuked the chaotic waters in the beginning time. Even late in the New Testament period, the Book of Revelation depicts water not only as lifegiving, but also as devastating: *The serpent vomited water from his mouth like a river after the woman, to sweep her away.*

Even against this grim background, however, water reaches its greatest dignity in the new dispensation. It cleanses the lepers; it cures the paralytic at Bethsaida. The compassionate Father in heaven *causes His rain to fall on honest and dishonest alike.* The waters of the Sea of Galilee form a backdrop for Jesus' breakfast epiphany on the lakeshore.

Gradually, though, water comes to mean "baptismal water," and gradually, all other waters are interpreted in the light of this new dignity. The Red Sea, Paul tells the Corinthians, was a symbolic model of Christians' baptismal water; and of the waters of the great flood, Peter says: *That water is a type of the baptism which saves you now.* So the earliest Christians dug deep baptismal fonts and went down into the waters—we go down into Jesus' death and rise from it—to come up alive in Christ Jesus.

We follow our Master, who went down into everything dark and dire in human nature and emerged victorious. Even in their depths, because of the great reversal wrought by Jesus Christ, the waters are now living waters.

The more staggering change in this symbolic "living water" is its source.  In the beginning, *the fountain of living water* is the Lord God Himself, as Jeremiah called Him, and the Psalmist.

Then came the fulness of time, the Feast of Tabernacles, when the people prayed for rain and commemorated the Rock at Meribah.  Jesus announced:  *"If any man is thirsty, let him come to me."*  Now Jesus is the source of living water.

But right then, Jesus worked another great change.  For he immediately extended to every one of His disciples what He had conveyed earlier to the Samaritan woman:  From the inner life of anyone who believes in Jesus *"shall flow fountains of living water."*  John adds the explanation that *He was speaking of the Spirit which those who believed in Him were to receive.*  We have received that Spirit.  Each disciple has become a source.

Well and good.  A source, a well-spring, of what?  At one point at least Sigmund Freud felt about the affluent people he dealt with in Vienna that their deepest selves were the source of every kind of vileness and  selfishness, more or less of necessity.  And Josiah Royce, an otherwise fairly optimistic American philosopher, felt us "by nature proud, untamed, restless, insatiable in our private self-will."  Do we think of ourselves this way, as though the deepest reality in us of itself produces wretchedness and evil, and not good?  Even if we escape this kind of conviction,  do we live afflicted by a lot of negative self-image and anomie, afflictions which seem part of our culture?

Standing against that cultural malaise, Christ's disciples believe that the deepest self of our selves wells up into desires and thoughts and actions that bring life, eternal life.  We consider this the achievement of God's Spirit in us, not of our own native forces.  But we also believe that our sinfulness and willfulness make that source sometimes ambiguous at best.  Here precisely we find an appropriate lenten problem.  We damage our selves as sources of life mostly by conscious habits of act and thought which violate our own consciences.  But we also comtaminate this deeply reliable source in more subtle ways, perhaps not poisioning the water, but fouling the taste and smell of it.

Thus, most of us would find ourselves more or less accurately categorized somewhere on a list like this one: fleeing obligations, uncommitted, refusing to forgive or to be forgiven, suffering repressions, unable to forget self for the sake of others. Or a list like this one: activism, hectic unrestraint, resigned sadness, aggressive self-assertion.

In a time when penitence is called for, we might remember that it is worth every effort to get off that list, completely, and to become more and more a very reliable source.

-------------------------------------------------------

All this raises important questions. The first rises from God's decision before we ourselves could make any decisions at all that we were to be deep sources of life and light to many in our own lifeworld. How do we accept that great gift with whole heart?

How do we accept those other definite persons whom God the Creator decided would be sources of life for us: our parents, for instance; the heroes of our day and its villains; those we fell in love with and those who fell in love with us? And who else?

Perhaps now we can examine the specific ways in which we—individually, as church, as great nation—have made our selves less than reliable sources.

-------------------------------------------------------

# Prayer

Lord, mighty God,
Source of all that lives and moves,
of all that changes and of all that remains,
You came into our own flesh
and became there the Source of our life and light.

And through baptism and the Holy Spirit,
You gave to those whom You had chosen beforehand
the gift of faith and divine love
so that now from within our humanity
gracefilled water wells up
washing us clean of all our sins
and nourishing in us the seed of eternal life.

Through Your Spirit working in us,
Through Your dwelling in us, Father, Son, and Spirit,
You make us the source of divine love
for one another,
and the accomplishment of hope,
and the instigation of peace.

Lord, mighty God, when we were unable to cleanse
the wellsprings of our own selves,
You plumbed all human depths,
and left there the sweet waters of salvation.

All praise to You, and honor and glory.

# 9. Looking for Reasons

*During His stay in Jerusalem for the Passover many believed in His name when they saw the signs that He gave, but Jesus knew them all and did not trust Himself to them; He never needed evidence about any man; He could tell what a man had in him.*

Why did Jesus suffer?

Most Christians recognize as blasphemous the ugly picture of God the Father demanding blood-revenge like a demented tyrant. We begin answering the question elsewhere today, in our own humanity.

First of all, we tend to think that Jesus had to suffer if He was to live the full human experience, as He indeed intended. The thought is easy enough to follow. Jesus was sent by the Father into human history. He came born of a woman, *in everything as human as we are,* and he went through separations and alienations, cuts and bruises, ugly surprises and failures and disappointments. He suffered all that. But He never sinned. He was to live and die *the Lamb without blemish.* So Jesus never suffered the scrambling of perception and desire that comes with sin, and the jostling of imagination and choice.

Then, are we to think that He kept always perfectly cool inside? Had He no problems with a death? No feelings of revulsion at a friend acting ugly? No anguish over failed love? What kind of human life would such detachment imply? None at all that any of us have experienced. And none that could be called *like us in everything.*

43

The matter is not simple, but Jesus did in reality enter into all of human suffering, including the suffering in our spirits. For if Jesus never suffered guilt and never confounded Himself by wanting with His whole heart two things at once, He was nonetheless essessutterly inculturated. He took into His emerging humanness all of the confusions, prejudices, violences, tyrannies, injustices endemic in His culture as in all cultures after sin. As He grew to realize how He had grown, He felt those confusions deeply. He was born during an imperial peace, but one that covered over conquest and preserved itself by violence. He was the citizen of an occupied country that yearned after its freedom because that freedom gave necessary evidence of God's fidelity to the Covenant. Yet His country divided against itself both physically and religiously. Jesus—*a carpenter's son* yet of unmatched brilliance—absorbed a culture seething with creativity, not in literature and music and architecture and painting, but in religion and rebellion. The young rabbi matured in a despised town—*Can anything good come from that place?*—in a region known for two things: sweet water from its inland sea and fervid rebelliousness from its over-religious population. A courteous and considerate man, astute and piercingly independent, a passionate lover—He suffered deeply from all the enculturated contradictions that He had introjected into His self while growing to the use of reason and to His own identity. He had to correct in Himself his culture's hatred of any Roman, disdain for any Samaritan, oppression of even its own women, and reliance on political means to reach religious ends. His human powers reached no further than ours do in making these corrections. Meanwhile, He suffered what was incorrect.

This raises a second thought about why Jesus suffered: The forces of evil battling in His polity and culture were personified, not abstract, and they struck Him down irresistibly and inexorably. Our thinking about Jesus' suffering can easily get abstruse, but the forces in His life were very direct and concrete. Who expects justice from a corrupt colonial governor? Or balanced judgment from an embattled clique? Or long memories in a mob? Even where political processes are ingeniously crafted, crafty geniuses twist them for partisan purposes. Especially where a people are deeply religious, religion is twisted to serve political purposes. *No wonder the prudent man keeps silent,* the prophet Amos snapped, *the times are so evil.* Jesus, however, found Himself driven to speak out, *"because that is why I came."*

Still, the force of evil is not greater than God. He could as easily have stopped human wickedness as His Son stopped the turbulence of wind and wave on the blue lake. Human evil, then, is not the whole explanation why Jesus suffered; it played its part because God the Father allowed it to.

Then did Jesus suffer because the Father willed it?

This introduces a third thought we often have, one close to scripture. The thinking is easy to follow, though we have to be bold to follow it and in fact, would not think along these lines at all except for revelation. *God did not spare His own Son,* Paul wrote to the Romans, but gave Him up to the benefit of us all. But Paul did not introduce this approach. Jesus Himself started it with the first prophesy of His passion. *From that time,* Matthew wrote, *Jesus began to make it clear to His disciples that He was destined to go to Jerusalem and suffer grievously.* He used the same kind of language much later on the road to Emmaus: *"Was it not ordained that the Christ should suffer?"* Now, to be *destined* to suffer, to have it *ordained* for Him, were ways of saying that God's will for Him was that He suffer.

Here precisely erupts the "scandal of the Cross": God does not merely salve humankind's sores and heal humankind's illnesses by a fiat from outside humanity; instead, He staunches its losses by entering into human powerlessness and filling it with His presence. "God made powerless" does not merely shock Jew and Greek and Wasp and Hispanic and everyone else; it trips very many down into disbelief. The cross does not merely promote unpleasant thoughts and dreams. The cross terrorizes people into turning their backs on God and on how God has chosen to create.

We need to pose the third question again. Are we to think that Jesus suffered merely because His Father willed it? Put that baldly, the blasphemy that we have rejected in our day leaps through. Jesus did not suffer merely because the Father wanted Him to suffer. That thought revolts any reasonable person. Yet Jesus *"came to do the will of Him who sent Me."* And in the garden, He put some opposition between His wish to escape His bitter passion and what His Father wanted done. We have to discover the way in which the wishes of the Father are involved.

We know a fourth way of putting these things together, more adequate if subtler and more complex.

Why did Jesus suffer? The Father wanted to save fallen humankind. But He meant not to force anyone to choose salvation; had He wanted robots, He would have begun creation Monday morning 8:30 with lasers. And had the Father forced each of us to accept salvation, He would not have saved us but transmogrified us into the strange clones that inhabit science fiction. Rather, the Father hoped to have this salvation come from within humankind. He hoped to have salvation elected according to its own freedom, out of love. God wanted humankind to choose to be able to love well, even perfectly, and that meant choosing to lay aside very, very much of what we know as familiar and even hold dear.

This wish itself seems nearly unimaginable: somehow, from within each and every human heart, a love for God and for others and for self would well up, passionate to its depths and splendid in elegant orderliness? Not very likely. We would never even have dreamed of that possibility on our own. That multitudes of people, from within our own shared humanity, would so love their lifeworld as to become together true children of the God of Love?

Yet, as we understand things, God could not allow Himself to be defeated in this wish, because the wish seems to be true to everything we know about love. But He faced the desperate disarray of all our forces. Who among us could do anything at all to straighten out the wreckage that follows our sin? Does any of us know what utterly selfless love even feels like, let alone how it acts? None of us has ever known how to get beyond our killing errors and mistakes, or how to get outside of our self-centered wishing and self-interested service to others.

Therefore, God sent His Son into this humanness of ours, clearly aware of two things. First: that His Son would indeed use His human freedom to love the Lord God above all, and then others—particularly those who seemed least to deserve special attention from the great—and He would love Himself wholly and generously. And second: that the rest of us would know how to restrain this heroism and do away with it.

Here again emerges the precise scandal of the Cross: The Son of God chose to take His stand exactly where two bitterly opposed forces cross—the selfless, passionate love of God for His free creatures, and those creatures' wrecked, inordinate love for themselves. *When we were still in our sin, He became sin for us.* In that crux, when no other thing and no other person could help Him, He cried out to His Father for mercy, and trusted love until He could not breathe another breath. So it came to pass that two loves killed Him: His own divinely faithful love, and humankind's tragically garbled love.

God's will then is indeed involved in Jesus' suffering. For God *wishes this perishable nature to put on imperishability and this mortal nature to put on immortality.* He has chosen that the vast wreckage of human freedom be salvaged and even glorified. Not by fiat, but from within the vast wreckage itself. His Son, Jesus Christ, has accomplished that great wish. But He paid dearly to accomplish it.

---------------------------------------------------------

Still, in the end these reasons why Jesus suffered do not shape up into an elegant geometric solution printed in the end of the book. They never will, and mature disciples continue always pondering the reasons. Why did He suffer?

And what can we say about the passionately loving Creator who chose not to salve human hurt and heal human brokenness by fiat?

And is it too much to ask that each of us look for reasons why we also should suffer *and so enter into glory?*

---------------------------------------------------------

# Prayer

Almighty and eternal God,
You alone of all that lives
know how to order what teems with chaos
and how to swallow up what is wrong and ugly.

You and You alone make the universes whirl and tumble
through all the unmeasured reaches of emptiness
around black holes whence nothing emerges.

And You come before the emerging suns
and reach beyond the ends of the uncharted galaxies.

In Your unfathomable wisdom, You have chosen
to leave darkness where You separated light from it
to countenance humankind's insolence
when we chose to set our own values
to leave us free still
even when we abuse ourselves and You with our freedom.

Most wonderful, You have chosen not to reject us,
and most wonderful, to unite Yourself to us as lovers do
in the Person of the Son
feeling with us our brokenness and arrogance,
embracing bravely everything dark and desperate
that we have inflicted on ourselves and on one another.

Lord, mighty God, when we are looking for reasons
why we suffer and why the innocent perish,
may we find there where He went on before us
Emmanuel, the One who came.

To this Hero be praise and honor and glory forever.

# 10. Just Anger

*You will all come to the same end unless you begin to reform.*

It requires a certain steadiness to ponder the two incidents that Luke alone records, a pair of small-group Armageddons. One happened up in the Galilee to a surprised group of religious zealots, whose *blood Pilate had mixed with their sacrifices.* The other had happened right in Jerusalem, an accident probably explainable by construction that was either careless to start with or ageing at the end, though how it was explained made little difference to *those eighteen who were killed by a falling tower in Siloam.*

The people who wanted to discuss the news of the slaughter in Galilee and the accident in Siloam asked a question that we have to extrapolate from the answer Jesus gave. *"Do you think,"* Jesus asked, because of their violent ends, *"that these Galileans were the greatest sinners in Galilee,"* and the dead in Siloam *"were more guilty than anyone else who lived in Jerusalem?"* To their questions, Jesus answered very clearly: *"By no means! Certainly not!"* But then Jesus went on to create a certain ambiguity: *"But I tell you, you will all come to the same end unless you begin to reform."*

*To the same end?* Not being cut down at an altar or crushed by a tower, surely? The way to prevent a death by political execution or civic malfeasance would be to get the ones who inflict it to repent, and Jesus was talking not to the powerful, but to people who feared dying such a

49

helpless death. By *the same end*, Jesus meant the kind of death His lis-
teners believed the unfortunate people had died:  a death at the hands
not of a politician or architect, but of an angry God.

Now here is where the required steadiness comes in.  Paul told the
Corinthians that these things were *written as a warning to us.*  In an age
that stresses the loving-kindness of God, can we hear a message about
an angry God?

The Jews of Jesus' day had no doubt that God could be angry, because although they had turned away from all idolatry, their God sat on
His hands while their Roman conquerers sat on His people.  They prayed Psalm 78, which notes God's anger a dozen times, an anger hardly
slight, for God *was enraged and utterly rejected Israel.*  They recited
Psalm 95, in which they heard God Himself exclaim:  *"Forty years I
loathed that generation..."*  The people knew this God, and it was of this
God that Jesus said, *"Fear Him."*

Today, we encounter certain theoretical problems in philosophical
theology about God and anger, which may hide too effectively the God
given us in divine revelation.  We really do have to wonder how an all-
loving God could be truly angry at those whom He loves.  How can
God, who must sustain in existence everything that is, love-it and not-
love-it simultaneously?  We face real mysteries here which our human
mind simply can not measure up to, as it simply cannot take the measure of the Name which the Lord revealed to Moses:  *"I AM."*  Nonetheless, that we do not find it easy today to think about God's anger
does not mean that it has evanesced.

In certain ways, our thinking is framed by our culture.  We tend to
stress the Lord of Life, for instance.  And of individuals,  our sense is
that the human person develops from an inner source.  We are optimistic in the expectation that the person who develops "authentically" will
quite necessarily develop holily and at one with God.  But our optimism
can deceive us.  It ignores God's revelation of humanity's collective sin,
on account of which each of us has introjected destructive disorders
(phobias, narcissism, bent sexualities, compulsions, addictions) into our
personalities before we ever make a single choice.  And in consequence,

as Paul told the Ephesians, *we live at the level of the flesh, following every whim and fancy and so by nature we deserve God's wrath.*

What is even worse, our optimism ignores the awesome truth that, quite "authentically," many choose darkness all of the time and all of us, quite "authentically," choose darkness some of the time. We postmodern Christians really do not like to entertain this dreadful possibility, than each single human person can freely choose a living death, in which every important action is intentionally destructive. We need to listen to Dr. Karl Menninger's probing question about whatever happened to sin. We have psychologized it out of account. But that does not mean that we have the power to psychologize it out of existence, and we are faced with the reality that some individuals act truly viciously and may well be electing a truly dreadful fate.

But can we think that God sustains the just person in her justice and the wicked person in her wickedness with exactly the same equanimity? Does God equally rejoice to sustain the liar in his lies and the honest man in his truth? Surely not, and yet the Lord of Life, *ordering all things sweetly from end to end*, must sustain human life even in its worse times.

Perhaps we have here a useful clue to the way an all-good, loving God gets angry. He does it this way: He simply gives to the evil what they are choosing, and that is His anger. So if anyone chooses to wreck his life and others' with drugs and irresponsible sex, God sustains that person in his choices--and those wrecked lives are God's anger. Perhaps the anguished self-doubt of the abused child is God's anger. And the burst bodies of terrorists' victims is God's anger. And the chemical poison in our water and the acid rain on our forests is God's anger.

Deliver us, Lord, from Your anger.

If we choose to make a neutron bomb, He will not hold in abeyance the mechnics of the subatomic universe in order to frustrate us. He will let us achieve our will—and we can reasonably think of that achievement as His anger. In this way, the just God lets us heap up our choices: the starvation of a Cambodian generation, the insane racism among American Christians, the political corruption in American life spawned by greed. It is precisely in every one of these madnesses that *the wrath of God is being revealed from heaven against the irrelgious and perverse spirit,* as Paul wrote for the Romans. And in this way we know God's anger among us.

Now it is true—we know from His own Son's life—that His anger touches even the innocent. The mystery of that ought not keep us from knowing that God Himself feels just anger. And we know from our own lives that those whom His anger touches through human sin and folly do not always know whether we are so innocent as not to deserve what we suffer, or whether we are so sinful as to deserve as much as we suffer.

But every human sin and madness provokes God and tests His patience. As we are touched by them, we need to remember Paul's warning: *Let anyone who thinks he is standing upright watch out lest he fall!* Or, to go back to those mini-Armageddons, let those who think they need not repent stay out of towers. They need no admonition to stay away from sacrifices.

-------------------------------------------------------

In any case, each of us might wonder whether anything in our lives could reasonably be called an experience of God's anger.

Could God be angry enough to let Hell mean having exactly and only what the totally self-centered have wanted—themselves?

God's anger, in the end, is the divine correlative of human refusals, and both have many degrees and kinds.

-------------------------------------------------------

# Prayer

Holy God, You have revealed to us

that Your love flares out in wrath and righteous anger

over injustice and infidelity and hate.

Even of those people who choose to violate others,

to wreck young lives or abuse wives or walk out on husbands,
even of those You are Source and Origin,
bringing them to light each day
and giving energy to their acts and thoughts and desires.
But You are not deceived;
from their own inner selves,
Your love raises up into expression in their lives
the punishing enactment of their selfishness,
and they are scorched in their spirits by their own breath.
Father of mercy and God of all consolation,
we acknowedge to You that we have provoked Your anger
in our own lives.
We have felt the weight of twisted love,
when sin is the penalty of sin,
and somehow even our sin is Your anger.
Lord of all compassion,
we fear that Your righteous anger
will leave us dead in our sin,
suffering what we have afflicted on ourselves.
Standing with Your own Son, whom You have given us in our flesh,
sweating in the remains of our wrongdoing,
we ask, Lord, have mercy.

# 11. Real Blindness

*"As long as I am in the world, I am the light of the world."*

The Gospel of John presents a long meditation on Jesus Christ. The theological themes of that meditation gradually came to maturity as an entire generation of disciples tried to live what He means and to ponder His meaning in the manner of Hellenized Jews. As if to underscore his theological seriousness, the author gets no closer to recounting a parable than the Good Shepherd and the Vine and Branches, which are rather metaphors than parables.

But readers who fear while reading the Prologue that their eyes are destined to roll back into their heads under the speculative weight are surprised to find themselves presently launched into stories. John tells stories one after another, chapter-length stories about real people like Nicodemus, Lazarus, the Samaritan woman, and the man born blind (the story in the gospel).

In the seven stories he tells in his first 12 chapters, John reveals more and more about Jesus. But he also means to reveal more and more about the men and women who encountered Jesus, because John sees in their experiences types and models of the experiences of later disciples who encounter Christ—not face to face on the streets of Jerusalem or at Jacob's well, but in the church and in the sacraments.

Thus, John means the church to see in the experience of the man born blind a type of our own experience of being born spiritually sightless, and in his encounter with Jesus, a paradigm of our encounter with Christ in baptism. Fortunately, John tells his story with such verve that we cannot forget that this man born blind was a real person, even if we do not know his name.

Will "Don Ciego" do? Generally, he gropes by as simply "The Blind Man," a moniker that offers two advantages: First, it seems to name a type rather than an individual and type is what John is after. And second, calling him simply "The Blind Man" underscores his sex which underscores the fact that in the Gospels no blind women show up. Does that mean anything?

Well, meaning is what we are after. But we will skew John's meaning unless we keep in mind while pursuing it that we are talking about a real human being. So, "Don Ciego"—or the half-dozen points of "meaning" get airy.

First. Though most of the people healed in the Gospel narratives come to Jesus for help, John has Jesus simply come across Don Ciego. He is stressing the gratuity of Jesus' gift of sight to the blind man, and he intends it to typify the gratuity of the gift of faith to all who believe. For the truth is that before any of us could argue with God in the tangle of our minds, He had already decided that He Himself would be our destiny, that we would come to Him through Jesus Christ, and that we would know all this through His gift of faith.

His disciples may wonder about His selection process, which of course is hardly as effective as we could make it. A lot of odd people do get baptized, and a lot of manifestly more deserving people do not. We might have an earlier type of this in David's selection. Samuel passed over the first seven of Jesse's splendid sons and asked for more, and then came David. *Samuel took the horn of oil and anointed him where he stood* (first reading). No one could challenge the fearsome prophet, and Jesse could only feel grateful. In the same way, our election to life in Christ is the subject of gratitude, not argument.

Second. In the ancient world, spittle was thought healing, perhaps somewhat like hot mud or brass bracelets in ours. So it may be that John meant nothing special in recording that *Jesus made a paste with spittle and put this over the eyes of the man born blind*, Don Ciego. But He was using a despicably ordinary thing as a vehicle of divine power. And then He told Don Ciego to go wash his face. So what's all that about?

It all typifies a point at which our supernatural baptism meets the Incarnation. We will find it necessary to use a lot of common, even scorned, means to live out our baptismal promises and *to try to discover what the Lord wants* (second reading). Inigo de Loyola wrote that once when he was trying to figure out what God wanted of him he would have followed a puppy if it promised to show God's will. Jesus had illustrated something of the same willingness by using mud patties. Have we put on His mind? We might find out if we examine closely whether we feel needs such as these: always higher forms of prayer, exquisitely tuned parish community, liturgies in the DeMille mode, or spiritual direction from the latest guru. Don Bosco and Francis de Sales and Catherine of Siena and a lot of other strong disciples considered puppies and mud patties a lot surer.

Third. Don Ciego's healing astonished everyone so much that he had to say repeatedly (even when his parents were trotted out to witness): "*I am the man.*" John the Evangelist made a good deal of this, and left no doubt how he meant to instruct the church.

God does not reveal to us our own sinfulness (which has its component of mystery) except as He reveals to us our living Savior. As we come to know that "*I am the man*," the one who sinned and sinned, the true sorrow of our response does not include sadness at our blind sin. If our sorrow comes from the Spirit of God, it includes the amazed, giddy lightsomeness of the man born blind, looking friend and foe in the eye—a miraculous source of data and comprehension—and repeating gleefully, "*I am the man. I am the man.*"

Until we truly accept His mercy, we are bound to deny everything, as those who were not very interested in mercy did to Jesus: *"We are not blind, surely?"* After we accept His mercy, which in a lot of ways is like letting Him rub spit on our eyes and cup our grieving faces in His warm hands, He lets us know just how blind we have been.

Fourth. When asked where Jesus was, Don Ciego said he didn't know. He had not gone looking for Jesus in the first place; Jesus had come and found him, as He comes and finds each of us. Only fools try telling God where to meet them. They die as blind as they were born. God decides where—in what kind of life, through what prayer and penitence, with what friends, upon what successes or failures—we will meet Him. Don Ciego's experience shows that He mercifully comes to where we are.

Fifth. The badgering of friends and officials led Don Ciego to reflect on exactly who Jesus is. His reflection stays close to what Jesus did in him: *"I don't know if he is a sinner: I only know that I was blind and now I can see."* His lead shows us an important way to grow in our Christlife: When we reflect on what He has accomplished and does accomplish in us, we come to real knowledge of Him. That knowledge sprinkles gratitude on the desert of our busyness.

Sixth. Don Ciego could see Him when Jesus came again, and that was a great thing. Still, he looked right at Jesus and asked about the Son of Man. *"Sir, tell me who he is so that I may believe in him."* Our experience is parallel here, too. Over and over again, as we let God draw us from sin and lead us into the *effects of light—complete goodness and right living and truth* (second reading)—we have to make an act of faith like Don Ciego's: This is the Lord; it is the Lord. In need, trial, joy, labor, every time He draws us to do the next good thing, we have to hear Him say, *"Do not be afraid. It is I."*

Standing in the light of faith, which mysteriously resembles a darkness, it is our happiness to have to do what Don Ciego did. *The man said, "Lord, I believe," and worshiped Him.*

---

A story can have many meanings. Don Ciego's intimate relationship with the Son of Man leaps from his story. In what ways does it typify the intimate personal relationship between any disciple and the Master?

And if Don Ciego's blindness afflicted him *so that the glory of God might appear*, why do our blindnesses afflict us?

What makes it possible for any one of us to say *Jesus is Lord*?

-----------------------------------------------------------

# Prayer

Lord God, You dwell in inaccessible light
that shines in perfect clarity through all that exists
but that we cannot see with our blind eyes,
as we cannot see radioactivity in charged rods.

You have chosen in Your kindness
to come to us where we dwell
in darkness and the shadow of death,
even to where we choose to wrap our darkness and death
wilfully around ourselves
and to avert our sightless eyes from Your gentle face.

You came to us, Lord Jesus, in just this way,
wiping away our sightlessness with Your own spittle,
wiping out our helplessness with Your own blood,
wiping away our cold loneliness with Your warm hands.

And for purposes we know are endlessly kind,
You have poured into our spirits Your Spirit,
endowing us with new light and even new life,
so that whenever we open our eyes yearning to see,
You give us to know Your glowing Presence
in universe and world
in event and circumstance
in beloved others and even in enemies.

We would live in that Presence, Lord mighty God,
so that when Principalities and Powers come
to ask whether we have been given sight,
and healed by the Son of Man,
we may answer, trembling in fear and in confidence,

"I am the one."

# 12. Lifted Up

*The Son of Man must be lifted up as Moses lifted up the serpent in the desert, so that everyone who believes may have eternal life in Him.*

It is an odd story about faith. The People of God get disgusted with desert living on dull food and the dry hope of water so they rebel against God. Suddenly, they find themselves ankle-deep in seraph serpents, whose deadly sting drives them to repentance. They ask Moses what to do and Moses asks God. The Lord commands him: *"Make a fiery serpent and put it on a standard. If anyone is bitten and looks at it, he shall live."*

The people kept this story alive and kept finding new meanings in it. Just a half-century before Jesus, the Book of Wisdom reminded them that those who gazed on the brass snake were saved *by the universal Saviour.* Early Christians saw very special meaning in that, remembering that Jesus had turned the story into an allegory.

Here is the allegorical interpretation of that odd story about faith: Jesus' disciples are those people wandering around the desert. The serpents are the consequences of our sins, which will leave us dead. The One raised up is Jesus. To look at the *fiery serpent* is to believe in Jesus. Although the model of the serpent brought no one to eternal life, everyone who looks in faith at Jesus *may have eternal life in him* (Gospel).

There is a further allegorical parallel, which is not as simply stated, but which tells us something vitally important about discipleship in Christ. For as the people actually wandered around a scorching desert being tested and proved by it, so do we wander around in our believing, being tested and proved by it.

The people were disciplined for wallowing in their disgust and acting unfaithful by being led for a long, long time around a desert, dying to self-reliance and to their pride. We, too, who have committed ourselves to belief in God and His Christ and their Church are disciplined for our immature and weak and faltering faith, and must die to our self-reliance and pride. Here are three points about that.

First. We who believe in God accept into our lives an impenetrable mystery, a One whom we will never in this life see or touch. We take this mystery and make it (or better, Him) the ultimate explanation of everything. We die then to the deep-seated human determination that raw human reason measure and encompass everything. We die to the prideful belief that our "science" can penetrate all existence and make meaning. We die to the existential arrogance of requiring that our lives make absolute sense in their own terms, without reference to an Other.

Instead, we turn to the One who was *lifted up*. Once again we have to die. We die this time to the prideful hope of explaining how a God came to be on a cross. But even bereft of explanation, we profess that our faith, far from being the dead intellectual freight and oppressive emotional baggage it looks like to the happily liberated, is a tremendous, unmerited gift. *We are God's work of art, created in Christ to live the good life* (second reading). Only a people with humbled spirits and contrite hearts can make that profession gladly.

Second. Our faith disciplines us in the way we understand *the good life*. Sometimes, we Christians sound as though we believed that the ultimate aim of faith in God were individual self-fulfillment and "authentic self-realization." In a certain very specific sense—one quite contrary to the sense accepted by our culture—we are correct.

What do we mean by *the good life*? Of course, human wisdom in every age teaches that true success cannot be adequately measured by social and economic achievement. The less-than-wise (and the wise on their off-days) feel fulfilled and authentic while driving this year's Z500-XL, wearing this year's cloth and colors and a massive gold chain, on the way to spend large bills at the Morning Gate Shopping Mall. The fulfillment intended by human folly turns presently to dust. But even the fulfillment intended by human wisdom ends in dust, if a little less promptly.

Faith in Christ Jesus confounds whatever we may mean by *the good life,* requiring of us that we accept a definition which is a promise, put in terms of a self-fulfillment which looks to the eyes even of the world's wise very much like self-emptying.

On our own, we simply cannot make a lasting *good life* for ourselves individually or for all of humankind taken together. For the true *good life* has been defined by God our Saviour in norms that transcend ourselves. Those norms are summed up in the One on the cross. So while we may not be much moved by the linguistically exuberant statement that when we suffer we are lifted up and *crucified with Christ,* that metaphor is nonetheless solidly rooted in the revealed Word of God. So is the reality; we do indeed *take up our cross daily.*

But we are slow to listen and to believe. For this reason, *the God of our ancestors tirelessly sends us messenger after messenger* (first reading). How do we receive these messengers from God?

Third. Those of us wandering around in our faith like the people wandered around the desert need to answer this question. Who are our "messengers from God," and how do we receive them? For the truth is that our commitment to Christ and the Church requires of us that we be docile. We learn what to think and how to think it from a guaranteed tradition. We must embrace the correctives of the magisterium, both bishops and theologians, even though having to accept correctives goes against our wish for autonomy, and having to accept specific correctives goes against our will to know already whatever we need to know.

Every American is full of culture-bound religious convictions and reactions, growing out of this nation's lively civil religion. Among other things, some Christians defend in biblical terms racism and sexism, and others, the arms race. We claim to listen only to the expert, yet the "religion" and the "morals" of all kinds of superstars figure importantly in the way we feel about our religious selves. Some repudiate weekly worship because they are "not turned on" by the liturgy, as though "getting turned on" were a moral imperative of greater weight than worshiping God. We substitute taxation for tithing and for personal presence to the poor. These and many, many more religious and semi-religious convictions and practices, we absorb from our culture.

But docility—an openness to accept instruction creatively—docility is not one of the traits we absorb from our culture. Somehow, we feel today that every important belief and conviction must rise up solely from within our own selves. We give tremendous honor to the individual's freedom, even when the individual is quite ignorant and sometimes when the individual is palpably perverse. Hence, if we are to believe wholeheartedly and well, we have to die to this excessive independence in the self. Not that we have to transmogrify into mindless fundamentalists; we know that the individual's conscience must continue the court of last resort. But we have honestly to admit that this court is too often very badly instructed and presided over by an ignorant judge.

So in our culture we die to ourselves when we accept seriously the obligation that our conscience be well formed, well informed, and well conformed. Try that one on a friend who has been deeply enthused by an M.B.A. or one too far seized by the enthusiasms of evangelicalism.

A conclusion. At times, our faith commitment can seem to turn our lifeworld into a desert. Then, this commitment and this desert impose on us a discipline, calling on us to raise our eyes to Christ on the cross. And in a very true sense, they lift us up in imitation of our Saviour. At those times, we need to keep in mind the double meaning of *lifted up*, since every act of faith we make is charged with the whole of it. In Jesus' experience, *lifted up* meant both crucified and raised to new life, both wrecked and renewed. When we gaze at Jesus on His cross, we are looking at our humanity utterly wrecked, for even the Saviour's humanity hung helpless on that wood. *He saved others, He can not save Himself.* But He rose, and that same humanity was lifted up to glorious life.

Now, in the measure in which our faith in God matches Jesus' faith in His Father, we too are lifted up. Right now, we feel the discipline of the desert a lot. The glory will come later. During these times when we feel the dying to our selves, we remember that in the same humanity that wounds us there dwells the power that raises us: Jesus our brother, Christ our Lord.

*For God sent His Son into the world not to condemn the world, but so that through Him the world might be saved.*

-------------------------------------------------------

In the end, then, we might wonder how Jesus' conscience was formed and informed and conformed.

How did He know—and how will we know—what of our culture's desires and designs and conceptions to cling to and which to struggle to escape from? To whom shall we listen?

How can we reconcile our own sufferings—the real, current ones—and our own self-fulfillment? We might wonder about that, too, when we gaze at the One who was raised on the cross.

-------------------------------------------------------

# Prayer

Lord Jesus Christ, when you were a child, and young,
You absorbed the great beliefs of Your people
and learned to love the law of the Lord.

You accepted with docility what the Law and its teachers taught
even as You learned not to do as they did.

You submitted to Your people's food disciplines
and followed the rhythms of their sacrifices and prayers,
learning how to hold on to what was good,
how to grow beyond what would trammel You
and imprison You in a culture of a time and place surely to die.

For Your devotion, You were raised up,
once cruelly by our sins,
and again gloriously by our God.

Now we raise our eyes to You, Lord Jesus Christ,
to learn how to cling to what is good in our lifeworld,
and to let go of whatever the Holy Spirit of Life
shall give us to know does not belong to us,
as You did through whom all the world is to be saved.

# 13. Come On, Celebrate

*But we had to celebrate and rejoice.*

The parable got a bad name as the subject of an early silent movie named "The Prodigal Son." The film lasted about thirty-three minutes, of which the first three or four presented the younger son taking his inheritance to a foreign land, and the last three or four presented the younger son repenting among the swine and flinging himself into his father's arms. All in between, of course, presented his *dissolute living* in rich costume and on vast sets, a pagan orgy with a cast of thousands. All that made the movie a come-on to identity with the deliciously wicked, readily redeemed, younger son.

During the past years, Scripture scholars have been observing—not that the parable does not really focus on the orgy—but that the parable puts the Loving Father at the center of events. Jesus truly intended to say as much about God forgiving as about sinners needing forgiveness. The father's deep grief that the son went off—lost to the temple, the Torah, and the close-knit family—is the dun field on which Luke's *celebrate*, a word he uses nowhere else in his gospel, stands out in summertime brilliance. *"We had to celebrate and rejoice! This brother of yours was dead, and has come back to life. He was lost, and is found."*

Jesus surely intended an insight into God's heart and mind here, just as He surely intended to make His hearers glad that the younger son's foolishness ended happily. The Lord is trying one more time to teach what He tried to teach every audience, that God's mercy is the greatest of His works, a truth we need to keep coming back to since it underlies any chance we have of eternal happiness.

The question to ask of the parable is, Who needs God's mercy? Jesus answers the question: not just the unfaithful, but even the faithful members of His household.

For as Luke tells the story, Jesus was addressing not only *the tax collectors* and sinners, but also *the Pharisees and the scribes*, who kept muttering to one another about Jesus that *this man welcomes sinners and eats with them.* Now these confident members of God's household were sinners just as much as tax-collectors and Samaritans. They just committed different sins. But like many of us they could not see it, and Jesus owed it to His Father's call to invite them to repentance. Actually, He had first of all to invite them to become sinners, or to put it another way, to see themselves as the sinners they were.

A lot of us are in the same fix. The truth is, it is fairly comfortable to empathize with the Prodigal Son, that scapegrace who at least had fun as he sinned, and whose story ends like a tearjerker. After Hollywood has its way with our self-image, we tend to project onto any Prodigal Son or Daughter a certain panache.

We do not consider it nice to empathize with the elder son. He dully stayed home, to start with. And he betrays the worst side of himself in the four scalding self-revelations Jesus puts in his mouth.

*"For years now I have slaved for you"* serves as his opener. The fact is, by Deuteronomic law, two-thirds of the father's estate would be the elder son's, so he was working for himself, as any harebrained heir would know. What's more, the younger son had shown a clearer perspective on life with father when he realized that even his father's servants lived well. So the elder son's *slaved for you* tells more about his feelings toward his father than about the objective conditions of his labor. His most obvious feeling is crabbed ingratitude.

Then he makes things worse when he snarls to his father that he, the elder son, *never disobeyed one of your orders.* Consequently, no doubt, he had never earned his father's anger, and probably never knew how to accept his father's quiet approval. It may be that we can see the man's point, actually; mere steady work merits no memorial day, and nobody much minds the spoke that fits in the wheel. But when we see his point, we see something else unattractive about him. His stance toward the father seems like one of legal subservience and not one of filial love. And what is more, he reveals in his remark a repulsively smug self-righteousness, an attitude that comes easy to the "already saved." His obedience was not so much a freely chosen way of joy as, sadly, the only way he could see to "freely" choose.

Naturally, that leads to deep resentment, and the third of his self-revelatory expostulations betrays the deep resentment that he is not automatically rewarded in ways that he, himself, considers appropriate. To the father he says: *"You never gave me so much as a kid goat to celebrate with my friends."* Not only no rich fatted calf, but not even a poor skinny goat! This biblical Narcissus, wrapped up in his dutifulness, cannot say that the father had refused him a calf or a goat. We certainly would have heard about that right now, wouldn't we? He seems plainly never to have asked. From this kind of father, who could believe a refusal? The ugly truth lies here: This son has never seen in the good things of his father's house reasons to celebrate. Celebration starts in joy and joy starts in gratitude. This lad never got a start.

His last snarl may be his worst, betraying what is perhaps the least attractive of all human vices, envy. His way of calling his brother *"this son of yours"* underscores his clear feeling that what his brother got, he got at the elder son's expense. This could hardly have been the case, as the Pharisees and scribes listening would well know, since the elder son was assured not only of his two-thirds inheritance when the father died, but was meanwhile sharing in his father's lifelong usufruct. But this elder son was clearly envious of what his brother had, and the father's response is a ferocious rebuke, scathing in its gentleness: *"My son, you are with me always, and everything I have is yours*" as long as I am alive and after I am dead.

Now in some real sense, we who are in the household of God's church are the elder sons of His new creation, and this story of the two kinds of children suggests that we need not contemplate absconding with the petty cash for a debauch in a neighboring state so that we can know God's loving mercy. We know it, even if our wickedness tends to the olive drab and not to the lurid scarlet. In our hearts, we keep thinking of ourselves as God's servants long after He has chosen to call us friends. In the church, we see our life as an obedience imposed, instead of as an invitation communicated by the Spirit within us. In our lifeworld, we treat our part of the earth like a stable, and it is the gift of a palace garden. And we keep competing, competing, with one another and with everyone in sight—as clear a sign of envy as a scratchy throat is of a cold.

So we can not ignore the father's response to the elder son's drudging life of sin. The response means much to us, and the father's loving reception of this son who was not acting very lovable comes as good news, too. Even faced with dull truculence and grating ingratitude, the Father keeps on inviting his child: "Come on in to the party, son. Come on."

-----------------------------------------------------------

In the long run, the elder son might harbor a bitter doubt under his shambling truculence. Can he, and we, feel certain that the father intends him nothing but joy?

And his failure to live both obedient and happy vividly raises this question: What motivation makes a person happy who *never disobeyed one of Your orders?*

But this parable, like all of Jesus' teaching, centers around God the Father, probing from every angle what kind of God has made Himself known to us.

-----------------------------------------------------------

# Prayer

Lord God, most prodigal Father,
You pour out every day all the gifts of creation
and fill our lifeworld with good things.

You give us faith in Jesus the Lord
and count us among those He calls friends.

You keep us safely in Your household,
and if You have not given us the gift of perfect observance,
still, You hold us by Your side
and in union with the people You love.

Lord of the riot of Spring and the romp of friendly minds,
You wait for the ugliness of all our orgies to end
and for the emptiness of our self-will
to fill with sorrow.

You are waiting when we turn back to You,
and then You prepare a party.

And, Lord, we want to come in.

# 14. Glory, Glory

*"I am the resurrection....and whoever lives and believes in me will never die." Do you believe this?*

Jesus, it seemed to some of Lazarus's friends, had unexplainably delayed and then come too late. He stood now at the cave's yawning blackness in the sweet stench of rotting flesh.

Everyone around Him had been consoling everyone else with the belief of the Pharisee party: Lazarus *will rise again at the resurrection on the last day* (Gospel). For over the centuries, the people had come to take as a promise of a real event to come something that the prophet Ezekiel had meant merely as an image of total triumph: *The Lord Yahweh says this: "I am going to open your graves, my people....And I shall put my Spirit in you and you will live"* (first reading).

Meanwhile, the stinking tombs threatened eons of dumb sorrow. Jesus stood there already knowing what He was to do. He had of course raised others from the dead—the son of the widow of Naim, the daughter of Jairus. But all of them had been barely dead, and everyone knew that the soul hovered around the body for three full days before going off for good. Lazarus was different; he was very dead. Not just what we today call clinically dead, either. Lazarus *had been in the tomb for four days already* and his cold remains gave off an unmistakable stink. Everyone around knew that he would have to wait until the rest of us were ready before he could rise again.

Jesus looked at the gaping hole. He knew what He faced: the confounding living process called Death. No humans beat it on their own—not one of us. Jesus knew also that the Father meant Him to nullify that process one more time so that He could bring Lazarus from the dark back to everyday light. He knew, finally, that this temporary triumph in his friend's life would bring down on Him the immitigable enmity of powerful people, who, reaching for another kind of temporary triumph, would kill Him. So Jesus knew very well that Lazarus's death and return to everyday life were to be tangled up, somehow inextricably, with His own death and return to another kind of life.

Can we fathom this? That an ordinary human life should be so entangled with the unique human life that wrought the redemption of the entire human race? We need to try, so that we can understand our own entanglement with this Jesus of Nazareth.

No wonder John recounts the story of Lazarus at length among the most symbolic incidents in Jesus' life. For the story carries the most awesome truths about Jesus Christ and at the same time the most central truth about our life in Him. These break into three points.

First of all, before and beyond all else, the story says that Jesus Christ is *life*. *"If anyone believes in Me, even though he dies, he will live, and whoever lives and believes in Me will never die."* So the nominal Christian—for whom the way is American, the truth is scientific and shifting, and the life is whatever we can get our hands on—knows nothing about the real Jesus Christ. Neither do cultural Catholics, the faithful who feel imposed upon by the Church's option for the poor, admonitions about birth control, requirement of weekly worship, and pleas against nuclear arms and against consumerism. All such "faithful" need to give steady attention to this truth: *"I am in the Father and you in Me and I in you."* They cannot have given much attention to it so far.

Those who do not have Christlife as the meaning of their human life will find no balance between the fulfillment of their self and the realization of community. Many who think deeply of it feel that the "self" has been emptied of unique content as people move in the lonely crowd.

Poets claim everyone wears a mask and psychiatrists muse that everyone fears intimacy. Journalists and novelists savage the human figure, because they perceive it as terminally distorted by various despotisms and technologies and scientific nightmares.

Those to whom God has given to know Jesus Christ, He has destined to hear the Saviour *crying in a loud voice, "Here! Come out! "* of all that chaos and madness into the light of order and meaning. Then at the end, all of us will hear the Christ say, on a summer day full of (perhaps astonished) friends, *"Unbind them, let them go free."* And we will emerge into a liberty such as only very secure children can now dream about. That will be *glory.*

But that is the last part of the *glory of God.* There is another *glory,* and it is the second thing that Lazarus's story illustrates.

Jesus asked Martha, *"Have I not told you that if you believe you will see the glory of God?"* Why *"if you believe"*? Even a casual passerby would have been able to see what happened. Lazarus had been loudly dead, and Lazarus walked out of his tomb trailing winding sheets and wafting odd fragrances. All around witnessed that with their own eyes, and many of them doubtless hugged him and listened to him tell his story. So why *believe*?

Well, Jesus constantly said that there is more to the *glory* than just the raising up. His own "raising up" was a complex symbol of power in defeat and of helplessness ending with the upper hand. A short time after He had raised Lazarus, he told the Greeks whom Philip brought to Him at a festival in Jerusalem: *"Now the hour has come for the Son of Man to be glorified. I tell you, most solemnly, unless a wheat grain falls on the ground and dies, it remains only a single grain; but if it dies, it yields a rich harvest."*

Even in His suffering and death, even in real defeat, Jesus was embodying and showing forth the Father's glory. For the time being, then, while we walk the path He walked among us, we will know God's glory in weakness and failure, in remissions and in dying to the self that is of earth. However, we will know that glory only *if we believe.* Later on we will know the glory of walking from the tomb like Lazarus, when we will no longer have to believe because we will see, and when all faith and hope are wiped away and only love endures.

Until then, do we fear death? Did Lazarus, after Jesus unwound him from the dark? Here is the third truth about life in Christ, which has to do with our own deaths.

Wise people, whoever they are, do not fear death though they may feel disappointed and angry at having to face it. Only fools fear death. They fear it so much that they try to deny it by what Paul calls the "unspiritual life" (second reading), that is, by living "the 'Dallas' syndrome." That denial of death is mad, mainly because the fear of death that gives it force is the wrong fear.

The thing to fear is not death. The thing to fear is living forever. Imagine that we do indeed live forever and live so badly that we would rather not live but die. That is the thing to fear: becoming such a person as will have to live forever badly. Forever, vague unease or pain; and forever and ever, loneliness. Now there is something appalling.

So even wise unbelievers "fear death" this far, that the thought of it moves them to live as though they will go on living forever. As for the disciples of the One who raised Lazarus from the dead, whether we are wise or not-so-wise, we scorn the denial of death. We even embrace death, whenever and however it is to come, for we expect that our Lord will be standing at the mouth of that darkness shouting down its arrogance in irresistible might.

Jesus Christ is, in the end, not only priest and prophet, teacher and king, and redeemer. He said it. In the end, *"I am the resurrection."*

----------------------------------------------------------

Still, when the story is told, when Lazarus is gone--when our grandparents and parents and friends are laid to rest--we are left with the question that haunts every human person: What does death mean?

Wouldn't anyone who expects to live forever have a distinctive attitude toward our present life and all its functions?

How do Christians experience God's *glory* in the hours and days when pain and failure and disappointment test us?

---------------------------------------------------------

# Prayer

Lord Jesus Christ,
most glorious Lord of Life,
in fear and trembling You went down into darkness and death.

Now no realm holds terror for You;
now no alien power can ever again touch You.

We who follow after You still walk in a valley of darkness,
in and out of the shadow of death.

We do not feel of ourselves any security
in the face of this loosening and loss.

We are so afraid of death
that we never let ourselves smell its sickly stench
and look at our corpses only after they have been painted
and dressed in street clothes.

But we sense that Your power hides even in this fear.

Your determination stays firm
even in our dissolution.

And by Your free gift,
gracious Lord of Life,
we look forward to hearing You call us forth
one day that the Father has already chosen.

We will come, Lord, naked and willing,
into Your kingdom with all Your friends.

# 15. Princely Paradigm

*During His life on earth, He offered up prayer and entreaty, aloud and in silent tears, to the One who had the power to save Him out of death, and He submitted so humbly that His prayer was heard.*

Sometimes Jesus talked about His passion as if it were to be the official fulfillment of prophecies, and hardly anything personal at all. When He said, for instance, *"The hour has come for the Son of Man to be glorified'* (Gospel), He was echoing Second Isaiah about the Servant of Yahweh: *See, my Servant will prosper, He shall be lifted up, exalted, rise to great heights.* Jesus' language at these times seems as ceremonial as Isaiah's. He sounds dispassionate, like a diplomat discussing the terms of a treaty (or a covenant).

But at other times, Jesus spoke with great and urgent feeling. Sometimes He spoke about Himself: *"There is a baptism I must still receive, and how great is My distress till it is over!"* Sometimes He spoke about others: *"I am going away; you will look for me and you will die in your sin."*

Speaking officially or speaking personally, however, Jesus was a single person. He prayed His own unique prayer; He had one attitude toward the Father. As He came to grasp what would happen to Him in Jerusalem at the Passover, His prayer developed accordingly. In fact, His prayer about His coming ordeal appears to have taken on a certain pattern. Jesus manifested that pattern in the public statements He made about His coming passion in front of crowds (Gospel) and in the intimate prayer He prayed in the garden, as well, with only His closest friends around.

There are four moments in this pattern of Jesus' prayer. The first begins when Jesus feels anguish as *the hour* draws near.

In front of the crowd, He said simply, *"Now My soul is troubled."* But when He entered with His three intimate friends into the garden, He let them see how *sadness came over Him and great distress,* as Matthew reports; and Mark adds that *a sudden fear came over Him.* Mark also records what Jesus said about His own feelings at that time: *"My soul is sorrowful to the point of death."*

Whether or not He revealed His anguish, fear, or sorrow, Jesus' prayer took its start in this experience. To put it negatively, Jesus did not demand of Himself that He set aside these experiences, or deny them, or arrange them rationally according to some philosophical principle, and then turn to His Father. He turned His face up to God out of the midst of anguish and fear and sorrow.

So, second in the pattern of His prayer, Jesus appeals to the Father for pity and help.

In front of the crowd, Jesus showed only that He had thought about asking the Father for pity. *"What shall I say, 'Father, save Me from this hour?'"* Yet, in telling a crowd that, He was letting them feel the resonance of the prayer in His heart; deep within, He wanted at the same time to beg God to be saved and to leave the entire matter in God's hands.

Alone in the garden with His closest friends, when the hour had arrived, anguish overcame any such confusion Jesus might have felt earlier on. Matthew and Luke report a prayer that seems to entwine anguish with restraint: *"My Father, if it is possible...if You are willing, take this cup away from Me."* But Mark, who wrote the Good News down before the others, remembers vividly that Jesus sounded like a boy calling out for his father. *"Abba! Everything is possible for You. Take this cup away from Me."* If we let the vibrant language get a little further from literal translation, Jesus said: "Oh, Dad! Dad! You can do anything. Don't let this happen to me." This is the only time known to us when Jesus Himself called on God as "abba—dad."

Third, Jesus humbly submits to death.

Before the crowd, Jesus expressed His submission the way a prophet might: *"It was for this very reason that I have come to this hour."* He showed His trust that even His suffering manifested the power of God at work in His life and in all human life: *"Father, glorify Your Name!"*

In the privacy of the garden, however, Jesus showed more directly the cost of His *submitting so humbly that His prayer was heard.* His prayer simplified: *"Nevertheless, let it be as You, not I, would have it."* And so did His anguish: *His sweat fell on the ground like great drops of blood.* The starkness of that suggests a reality of His and of all human experience. At a certain point, there is no more to be said and no further contest. The thing is to be done.

Fourth, the pattern of His prayer ends when Jesus receives some response from the Father.

In front of the crowd, the response was at times *a clap of thunder* or perhaps an *angel speaking to Him.* Jesus knew that it was the voice of His Father speaking *"not for My sake, but for yours."*

The response in the privacy of the garden was quite different. Luke mentions that *an angel appeared to Him, coming from heaven to give Him strength,* without suggesting that the angel brought anything like comfort or peace—just strength. Matthew indicates no answer at all. Nor does Mark, except to report that Jesus returned to His friends and said: *"It is all over."* In a certain sense, that was the answer He received from the Father: the decision to do what He knew He wanted to do. Every hesitation, every reluctance, every dread, He was enabled to set aside.

Those are the four moments in the pattern of Jesus' prayer before His passion. Actually, within these four moments, there seems to lie another pattern. Twice, a moment of clarity is followed by a moment of ambiguity. Thus, the hour is clearly drawing near; Jesus knows it is coming and can not doubt it. But then He feels this doubt, this ambiguity: May He ask for deliverance or not? Mustn't He feel delicately what the Father's situation is, and ask for deliverance only if it is "possible"?

Then He reaches another moment of clarity: He firmly accepts whatever is to come as from the Father's hand. He sets aside the ambiguities over what He can or can not, should or should not, pray for. He will simply embrace what is coming. That then leads another time to ambiguity: What is the Father's response? Thunder, a voice, silence? We may feel that the message, "Be strong and endure this excruciating situation," seems no message at all, coming as it does from the One who can clear up the situation Himself. But clearly, Jesus was able to accept as a loving response from His Father the strength to endure. What seems profoundly instructive here is that Jesus goes on to His work only strengthened, not, as far as we know, clear-minded beyond ambiguity. He died trusting God, as every one of us must.

Serious disciples will etch on their hearts the four moments of Jesus' prayer to His Father as He faced His passion: the acknowledged anguish as the time comes, the plea for pity, the humble acceptance, the faith that the prayer is heard. It is a paradigm, princely and perfect. And its great point, plain in Jesus' entire life, is that what matters is the deed willingly done, and not the way we feel about it.

------------------------------------------------------

In the end, it seems astonishing that we know this about our Lord and Saviour: *During His life on earth, He offered up prayer and entreaty, aloud and in silent tears.* Can we see how He acted with great courtesy to let us know, when many would have kept their own counsel?

In what ways are we to imitate His great courtesy?

But who would have thought that we could be asked to imitate even Jesus Christ's prayer?

---------------------------------------------------------

# Prayer

Lord Jesus Christ,
You did not think that You had to cling
to Your majesty and power.

Instead, for the sake of Your own love,
You poured Yourself out
and ended like a hard-used slave.

Even when You faced being cut off
and thrown out by false men and their lies,
You did not let them make You doubt
Your self or the Father's love,
or demand that He prove His love by saving You.

Gentle Lord,
You fell down in Your anguish
and pleaded with Your Father.

Teach us to pray as You prayed
so that everything appears to us as it appeared to You,
as coming from His hand.

# 16. Something New

*I wish to know Christ and the power flowing from His Resurrection.*

As had happened often enough, Jesus was in a bind. He had hardly come from Olivet to the temple in the early morning when some religious leaders threw at His feet a woman *caught in the very act of committing adultery.*

He faced a genuine dilemma. If He told them to go ahead and stone her as the Mosaic Law clearly prescribed, He would be answerable to the Romans, who reserved to themselves the power of life and death. And even if He could expect to finesse prosecution by Roman authority, He could not finesse His own authority. Hadn't He lectured them emphatically: *"Go and learn the meaning of the words, 'It is mercy I desire and not sacrifice'"*? On the other hand, if He told them not to stone her but to let her go, then He would be flouting the law and the prophets, and He had recently proclaimed just as emphatically: *"I have come, not to abolish them, but to fulfill them."*

Anyhow, that's what Jesus' dilemma looks like to us now. We might not be reading the situation perfectly, but it doesn't really matter in the last analysis. For Jesus found a way out of this human bind without running over anybody, as He always did. He listened to the leaders. He gazed at the woman. Then, without a word, He began tracing His finger through the dust.

81

It's the only time Jesus is said "to write," anything, and what He actually did has provoked endless speculation from St. Jerome on. But whether He named the capital sins of each scribe and Pharisee, starting with the oldest, or drew mystical signs comprehensible to only one and then another—whatever He did, He effectively shifted the accusers' attention from the guilt of one wretched person to the judgment every human faces. In consequence, they *went away one by one*, until, as St. Augustine put it, there were only two left, Misery and Mercy.

We could do worse than be with this woman, Misery, for a moment, and let three or four thoughts chase one another through our heads.

First, the gentle teacher who shows patience and compassion to both accuser and accused is the same person of whom the Baptist had said, *"His winnowing fan is in His hand."* He is the one who, on the day already assigned by the Father, *will sit upon His royal throne and assemble all the nations before Him.* For, as He said Himself, *"the Father Himself judges no one, but has assigned all judgment to the Son."* Has He passed judgment? Well, did we look at ourselves honestly, we would note that the final discrimination between just and unjust does not appear to have come yet.

Hence a second thought: Whatever this judge does right now, He will wield His winnowing fan only in the end time, on the Day of the Lord. In the interim, He has not chosen to make unarguably clear who of us are sheep and who goats. This means that no one of us can any more justifiably cast the *first stone* than any of that woman's accusers.

Even closer to home: We do not know for sure about ourselves. We have to recognize that whether we are justified before God is a mystery, not known finally during a lifetime. No one of us knows with metaphysical certitude that he or she will live forever with Christ's life. That's exactly the point of living by faith, and of having the great promise in hope only.

Paul put it this way for the Philippians (second reading): *It is not that I have received it yet, or have already finished my course, but I am racing to grasp the prize if possible, since I have been grasped by Christ.*

Here a third truth comes crowding in on the second. All of us who believe in Him in more than word, who have accepted the consequences of our saying *Jesus is Lord,* have first been *grasped by Christ.* We have the first sign of our salvation in our election to the human minority who know Jesus Christ—not just as an interesting historical figure, but living in the Church. We will be able to interpret that sign in the extent to which we comprehend that we did not choose Him, He chose us.

In fact, the whole of humankind has been seized by Christ, and so He has already judged the world. As He said: *"Now has judgment come upon this world, now will this world's prince be driven out."* He said now?

Now. Here is the fourth thought: Jesus Christ judged humanity by taking human nature into union with divine nature. He thereby passed the definitive judgment on death and on sin that lies at its root. He decided that humankind would not dwell eternally in grey shadows, but would live eternally in enfleshed spirit.

We did not have it in us to raise ourselves to a fully human life transcending earth's little time, but were doomed by our sin to death and to an immortality without the resurrection. The Greeks had it right: In the human cosmos they knew, each of us was so created that we would be immortal, but immortal only as a "soul." Each was fated to live and die and then to live forever in a kind of shadow world. The Greeks called it Hades, the place of the Shades of the Dead.

Then came Jesus of Nazareth. The Son of God, in His own self, destined humankind to integral human life, and achieved it. With the accomplishment of His life *("It is finished")* and Resurrection, He restored humankind to full human immortality as enspirited flesh. That is the judgment. So now there can be only those who so live as to stand with Christ and those who so live as to stand over against Him. All of us who live after Christ choose life or choose death.

He is a springtime come to a frozen wasteland at the north, the mere fact of whose coming means the onset of life and of flower. This springtime is already come, for the judgment went against death, and life is stirring in the cold dark. God's presence in humanity goes beyond the promises of Abram's seed and a kingdom merely of milk and honey.

This is what Isaiah dimly foresaw (first reading) as *something new.*

We need to recall it when life slams us down before the Lord Jesus like the woman snatched from the sinful act. We are all snatched in every sinful act; God does not need messengers or witnesses but holds us, even sinning, in the palm of His hand. Before Him, we come to know why Paul *accounted all else as rubbish, so that Christ may be my wealth and I may be in Him, not having any justice of my own based on the observance of the law.*

Like that woman, Misery. What justice did she have, based on anything at all? As the judge forgave her, so He forgives us: for no reason other than His loving mercy. We do not first make ourselves holy and then turn to this Lord.

He made Himself sin and He came to stand among the accused. In judges, that's *something new.*

---

All these considerations confront us with a profound question, how Jesus Christ can at the same time save and judge us.

And if Jesus has already judged us, how are we to judge ourselves?

Has all this anything to do with the petition He taught His disciples to pray: *Forgive us our trespasses as we forgive those who trespass against us?*

---

# Prayer
Lord Jesus Christ,
every person You looked at, You loved,
like the Father,

who loves the good and the bad, the just and the unjust alike
even while He loathes the sinner's sin.

You wished to gather into Your love
those who knew anguish and those who knew confidence,
all who wielded power and all who were oppressed,
the great and the little, the smart and the dim,
so that every one who walks the earth as You walked it
might have life, more and more.

Though the fouled relationships of those around You
with their selves and among themselves
with You and with their God
cut You out and cut You down,
You came back to live in our flesh.

Lord, if You will give us Your Spirit,
we mean to walk Your way.

In each person around, we choose to see
the passionate making of a passionately loving God,
in those whom we love and in those whom we dislike,
and especially all who live misery,
lying wounded in the world's ditches,
starting with our own self.

# 17. Civil Order

*Then they spat in His face and hit Him with their fists.*

How could it happen that the most civil of all men should die in a frenzy of savagery? Even in the end, He remained as civil as a Persian prince on a sunny hillside with friends sharing bread from a basket. Jesus' serenity above the bloodlust of the earth around Him was like a cloudless dawn rising above a battlefield.

He celebrates Passover with His close friends and the orderly ceremony is traduced by an intimate who has plotted betrayal and will end in a suicide. He goes with His closest friends out into an evening garden, not to carouse away from any who might protest, but to commune and to pray. Into the silver quiet of this olive grove explodes *a large number of men, armed.* Jesus' violated civility emerges in His indignant question: *"Am I a brigand, that you had to set out to capture me with swords and clubs?"* He will neither let His own men fight for Him— *"Put your sword back"*—nor call the Lord to breach history and save Him. He was Himself God's breach into human history, a breach no more violent or uncivil than the birth of an infant, or earnest talk among friends.

So He stood numbed, a man whose friendship had cooled fevers and staunched bleeding and made the mad sane. He stood numbed while one *whom I had called my friend* subverted the most civil of signs, a friendly kiss, and made it into a sacramental of savagery.

In the brief colloquy of that embrace, Jesus said, *"My friend, do what you are here for."* With that line, Jesus summed up how utterly His heart and soul filled the ways of humankind with divine civility.

Civility is not a smooth veneer over gnarled turmoil. In culture, it structures order into social consciousness and elicits harmony of interests. In individuals, its orderliness and harmony marshal emotions, conceptions, and desires as well as actions. And then these give ease in self-restraint, readiness to reach out in self-donation, and gratitude in both continuity and change.

Jesus of Nazareth lived, in every sense, civil. He learned that from the Father, from whom He received everything. For the Father, the God of all gods, acts with total courtesy towards all of the reflective beings He has created, never forcing love upon any of them. Jesus brought this divine civility and courtesy into humanity.

No civis Romanus, though privileged to live the Pax Romana, He was born into a culture whose people were civil toward one another, when they were, because their God's holiness required it. He absorbed His people's civility and enlarged it, reaching out to Samaritans, for instance, which others found unfeasible; and granting Caesar's to Caesar; and healing with a touch a servant's cropped ear. His self-restraint worked so manifestly that those who seized Him knew that they bound Him by His leave.

Then why was His end so savage, shot through not only with cowardice and duplicity, but also with fists and spit and splashes of blood? The reasons lie deep in the lives of those who put Him to death, with parallels deep in our own lives.

For if civility is none, neither is savagery merely a veneer. It is first of all an eruption of profound personal and social insecurity that endues everything with vehemence. True savagery is not haphazard but altogether purposeful. It is a concatenation of iron imperatives which link personal and social actions into destructive chains of violence.

Well, Jesus faced two insecure authorities, imperial and religious. Considered apart from their insecurity, they were each ultimate authorities in their order, and neither was any more steeped in civility than they generally have been or are now. Given the insecurities of Pilate and of the Sanhedrin, they could hardly have acted civilly under the pressures brought on them by Jesus of Nazareth.

His religious leaders felt the insecurity of having known no prophet for two centuries (which certainly calls for our compassion). They had split in contention over as fundamental a matter as the resurrection of the body. Their high priesthood was Rome's plaything; their political life, so tightly braided into the righteousness of the covenant, was rendered inane by conquerors obsessed with centralized control.

And yet that imperial force lived equally insecure, particularly upon the restive Jews who had rebelled before and promised to rebel again and again. Pilate had already *mingled Galileans' blood with that of their sacrifices,* and would later cut down a whole procession of Samaritans at Mt. Garizim, he was so fearful of the people.

If Jesus was trapped between religious and imperial insecurities and was to be destroyed by their savagery, so was Judas. The difference lies in this, that Judas himself turned savage, while Jesus kept His civil course. In the clear order of Jesus' mind, and in the purposeful commitment of His spirit, what Judas had come into the garden to do *would fulfill the scriptures.* Most of us would see it much more darkly. But in any case, as Jesus saw it, *this is the way it must be.* The savage construes every violence as necessary; the civil construes whatever is necessary as an occasion of grace.

At no juncture in His life was His grace-filled civility more plain than in His last hours as they unfolded in a nightmare of savagery. The One who had wanted only to be a vine joined to its branches was crowned with a thorn-vine and made to carry a lethal branch to which He was fixed with nails. People just passing by inexplicably turned on Him, *jeered at Him, shook their heads* and shouted, *"If you are God's son, come down from the cross!"* It is chilling that, by their own admission, they remembered that He had *saved others*. Their terrors were so deep that they could let His mastery mean nothing to them.

So He hung on the cross. But if His enemies' savagery had driven them to whatever they thought necessary for the good of the people, His civility had given Him freedom to choose. *For my part, I made no resistance, neither did I turn away. I offered my back to those who struck me, my cheeks to those who tore at my beard. I did not cover my face against insult and spittle* (first reading).

This is quite beyond what we know as nobility in human nature, for Jesus brought to this clash something altogether beyond what we know. *He did not cling to His equality with God, but emptied Himself* (second reading). Then, He had been God's equal, filled with a Self which predates the hills of Rome and the schist deep under the temple, and under Calvary.

Unlike those crucified with Him, unlike the rest of us, *who are paying for what we did,* He was wholly and innocently civil from His first day until they rolled the stone across His tomb.

On the face of it, the whole affair has all the marks of unspeakable waste.

---------------------------------------------------------

In the end, we will not understand Jesus's victory unless we comprehend how, in some very real sense, the savagery of His enemies defeated Him.

Do His thirty-odd years of life seem a waste? They were nonetheless the most productive of any human years.

Taking the "natural" as what we see with sophisticated eyes, we could contend that Jesus of Nazareth did indeed die a natural death. That would imply some stark things about human society and what it needs from His disciples.

---------------------------------------------------------

# Prayer

Spirit of the living God,
it was through Your power that Jesus was conceived
and born of the gentle Virgin Mary,
and under Your guidance that He went into the desert
and learned how to live truly Himself
and what He had been sent to do.

Lord, You held Jesus of Nazareth together
through the searing strains of betrayal by friends,
through bitter judgment by deceit and duplicity,
and through the mindless brutality of trained executers.

Lord of all that is civil,
You breathed into Him that same spirit,
in which He remained silent through the savagery of His end.

We feel confounded
by His horrifying sufferings
and by our own pain and grief
and by all the dreadful wreckage of our lifeworld.

If You please,
Holy Spirit of our most courteous God,
hold us together,
each one and all of us,
in Your divine civility.

# 18. Haunting Questions

*"Do you ask this of your own accord, or have others spoken to you about Me?"*

During the dark hours after they had laid Jesus' body to rest in the living rock, His disciples were haunted by doubts and questions. These questions of theirs have not been written down for us, but we do not need that. We surely know what they asked themselves. Why had they all run away? How could Peter have denied Him? Why hadn't the Father saved Him? How could any of this have happened to their friend?

Even after they had seen the cycle completed of *His raising up,* and even after they had come to admit that He had at the very least allowed these events to happen to Him, they continued to be haunted by questions. So when they began the task of ordering all their stories about Jesus—they shaped the story of His passion first of all—they left in their account of the last few days in Jerusalem a notable number of queries, put by friends, by enemies, by Jesus Himself. In reporting these queries, they seem now to have symbolized how they had questioned themselves over and over again, driven by grief and self-accusation, even after the Lord had been glorified.

We are haunted by our own questions when we read the account of Jesus' passion. But when we attend to the queries embedded in that account, we find them helping us realize a crucial truth: We do not question the events of those last horrifying hours. Rather, the events question us, just as they did the first disciples who could not forget them.

*Why this waste?* Looking back, those who *indignantly asked one another* that question must have felt that a great water jar of precious ointment would not really have been too much. They repeated the story of the alabaster box at Bethany, wondering why they had not grasped that the woman was *anointing His body beforehand for its burial,* even when He told them. But their minds were not prepared for all that waste.

*Where do You want us to go and make the preparation for You to eat the passover?* Looking back, they wondered at how straightforward it had seemed, just one more ceremonial dinner. But later, it seemed as though His simple gesture that final evening had transformed a starving city under siege into a town with windows and gates thrown open, eating well through the summer and waiting for a rich harvest from its free countryside. For they came to understand that the Supper had been His way of making them know that He forgave them from the heart, as if He had been anointing them beforehand. *Until the Lord comes, therefore, every time we eat this bread and drink this cup, we are proclaiming His death.*

But for a while at first—if they act at all the way we act—their proclamation was not without a certain ambiguity. Each looked back to moments of weakness and helplessness that seemed to expand and engulf all other times.

*Not I, surely? They were distressed and asked Him one after another.* When they looked back, they felt no anger against Judas. And toward Simon Peter, they felt nothing but great compassion and unhesitating loyalty. True, Peter had been the one to disown Him *three times.* True, Peter had pulled Jesus to himself with handfuls of tunic and, voice straining in bottomless anguish after Jesus' prophecy of the coming triple denial, had squeezed out this: *"Even if all lose faith, I will not."* But something else was true. When they all looked back, every one of them wept to remember: *They all had said the same.*

*Are you asleep? Had you not the strength to keep awake one hour?* Peter, James, and John could not believe that they had dozed; the supper had not been so besotting. They had let sadness dull them. But He had so often spent the long reaches of the night in prayer like this that He seemed simply to be going His own way, no matter how menacing events had become. They had not let the differences in this night's appalling darkness touch them, until His next query cracked out.

*Who are you looking for?* He asked this to his enemies' faces, not hesitating for a single breath. He knew whom they were looking for. They knew He knew. But the force of His authority shattered each enemy's resolve, and they had to fall together as a mob before they could lead Him away.

*Are you the Christ, the Son of the Blessed One?* Jesus answered that for the Sanhedrin, though for the most part He moved through the long hours in deep silence. He refused to dicker with *that fox* Herod or to debate the pretentious Pilate. He did answer directly one question that Pilate asked: *Are you the king of the Jews?* But He stayed silent when Pilate pressed on: *Where do you come from?*

No one could really answer Pilate's most ironic question: *Why, what harm has He done?* What harm, indeed. This good man, this sweet rabbi, this tender prophet. A hundred protests must have screamed in their blood—in the blood of everyone there.

The last query in the Gospel story of His passion is asked by Jesus Himself. Later, thinking back on it, those who had been too afraid to stand with His mother under the gibbet remembered this question as one of those things that went farthest toward healing their self-despising and the grief that they had been so useless to their friend. The disciples knew the whole of Psalm 22, from which Jesus took the query. The psalm begins in anguish and ends in affirmation, starts in despair and ends in hope. But when they told the story of His passion, the disciples recalled only the beginning of the psalm, just a single verse of it, for a startling reason. In Jesus' dying question, to their absolute astonishment, His disciples found themselves in company with God the Father.

*Eloi, Eloi, lama sabachthani. My God, My God, why have you deserted Me?*

It seemed in those dark hours that the Father, too, had deserted Him.

How did He come to be so alone, then, this dutiful Son and faithful friend? How did He come to be left by everyone—so patient and resigned, so completely naked to His enemies?

---------------------------------------------------------

In the end, any disciple who stands on Calvary under the cross of Jesus feels the whole self resonate with questions.  Would I have run away with the rest of His friends?

Would I have remembered all the questioning?

Do I remember much the whole grievous story?

---------------------------------------------------------

# Prayer

Lord God of tenderness and truth,
You ask of man and woman, 'Where are you?'
and You ask, 'Who told you that you were naked?'

You ask, but You know.

We are hiding from You in the garden of our desires,
and we have told ourselves our nakedness.

Loving Father,
You never had to ask 'Where are you?'
of the One You sent into this garden of our desiring.

From them who left out nothing that might destroy Him—
scorn, scourging, betrayal, treachery, bloody death—
from them before whom He hung utterly naked,
He hid the power that He shares with You.

But from You, even opaque to Him in the end,
He hid nothing, but lived utterly transparent.

In Him, even hanging a bloody lump of death on a cross,
You never saw anything but glory.

See, Father, even while we try to hide ourselves from You,
see this same glory in us,
who live naked before Your just and holy gaze
in Christ Jesus our Lord.

# 19. The Power of God

*"I have prayed for you that your faith may never fail."*

Dense mysteries surround the cruel death of Jesus. Like clouds hiding on a mountaintop, they make contemplating His passion difficult and give us excuses for putting out of mind the truth that God's Son, *being born in the likeness of men, humbled Himself, obediently accepting death.*

Even aside from the mysteries, we find it hard to think about His passion. We are repelled by the violence and the injustice. We are reminded of our own death, and of the truth that *not even the just have here a lasting city.* And we are instinctively chary that those who think of *what Christ suffered in the flesh,* as Peter wrote, are drawn to *adopt His same mentality* to submit to anything, to suffer anything, required by love. We find that fearsome.

In Christ's passion, we find vividly present certain mysteries that confront us all the time, mysteries that we would just as happily put out of mind. To begin with, the mystery of suffering itself: Why is there any cross at all, not just for Jesus of Nazareth, but for any human person? God is both almighty and all wise; why are there droughts in the Sahel and earthquakes in Turkey that wreck lives? How can the good God call to life and sustain in life men like Joseph Stalin and Pol Pot and Idi Amin, who through stupidity or viciousness or both blast the lives of tens of thousands? The questions are so urgent and so unanswerable that some find it easier, standing knee-deep in the wreckage humankind has made of things or the wreckage humankind finds falling around its head, not to believe in God than to acknowledge His lordship. Those

**95**

who find the alternatives—unbelief and belief—both unpalatable might just as soon not contemplate the human wreckage of Jesus' passion and be reminded that they must make a deliberate choice.

Even if we have made our peace with the imposing litter of humanity's world, we find another dense mystery surrounding Jesus' suffering. For He lived an innocent life and died innocent, reminding us of the fact that many—some—any one at all—suffer innocently. What is the just God doing as children starve in Kampuchea or come to life infected with AIDS because of their progenitors' irresponsibility? Is God at the birth of a moron? How is it possible that He even seem to forsake Him who can cite Psalm 22 with entire justification: *"To you I was committed at birth, from my mother's womb you are my God"?*

Both of these—the plague of human misery corroding the planet and the suffering of the innocent—are true mysteries, matters which are beyond our mind's capacities. They are mysteries that Christ's followers face in company with all humankind.

But inside them, as it were, hangs *Christ Himself, who died for the guilty, though He was innocent.* So within the awful mysteries of cosmic suffering and suffering innocence shelters another mystery, altogether stupendous: This outcast is the anointed Redeemer sent us by God.

Every person who hears Jesus' story confronts Him dying, and must ask whether he or she can believe this is the Redeemer. Many, many are scandalized by Jesus' death and cannot believe. The very good and loyal man, John Adams, for instance, wrote late in his life that he could not believe that God would "come down onto this ball of mud to be spat upon." And many others, even professed disciples, find it nearly impossible to gaze long on a crucifix. These are all scandalized, as Jesus Himself predicted many would be.

The scandal exploded fullblown when the Sanhedrin stood Jesus before themselves and demanded of Him: *"Are you the Messiah?"* Jesus said, as Luke records it, that He was the Son of Man, and that as had been foretold He would from then on *have His seat at the right hand of the power of God.* The Sanhedrin—71 elders, priests, and scribes—understood what Jesus was saying about Himself with this answer. *"So,"* they pressed, *"You are the Son of God?"*

Now they did not mean exactly what we mean by the expression after nearly two millennia of theological reflection. But the title *"Son of God"* had a consecrated usage in the Law and the Prophets. The *Son of God* was the specially chosen one, the scion sprung from David, the King of whom God said through the prophet Nathan: *"I will make his royal throne firm forever. I will be a father to him and he shall be a son to me."* The *Son of God* was to be a figure of power and brilliance, the one through whom Yahweh Elohim would fulfill His great promises to Israel. He was to embody the saving *power of God* and in His own person make the redeeming *glory of the Lord* shine upon all the people.

Jesus stands in front of them, hands tied, face blotched from fists and slick with spittle, and claims to be that powerful, brilliant *Son of God.* This peripatetic beggar, the manifestation of the *power of God?* Then God is a powerless nothing. This battered zealot, the incarnate *glory of the Lord?* Then God's glory is darkness. Manifestly, Jesus' claim to be the chosen One, the Son of God, was a ferocious insult to the Holy God, a blasphemy. *"What need have we of witnesses? We have heard it from His own mouth."*

Thus Jesus becomes, as Peter put it, *the living stone rejected by men but chosen by God and precious to Him,* precious too *for you who are believers.* Still, if the Sanhedrin were scandalized that a pathetic beggar could personify the glory of the Lord, perhaps we are scandalized that the risen *power of God* moves among us like a powerless beggar.

We believe that Jesus rose from the dead, and after ascending to the Father, poured out His Spirit upon the Church. We believe that this "pale Galilean" *not only died for us—He rose from the dead, and there at God's right hand He stands and pleads for us,* as Paul wrote to the Romans. We believe that His *power is at work* in us to accomplish great things in us.

But we tend to ourselves to be so little. We seem to agree with many nonbelievers that what we experience as our negligibility constitutes our true selves. We feel quite entirely negligible. We are very likely to feel that *the salt of the earth and the light of the world* might well apply to Mother Theresa and Pope John Paul II. As for ourselves, we feel rather more like a compost heap than the salt of the earth; more like a dead drycell battery than the light of the world. When John the Presbyter calls us all *the saints,* we are inclined to appreciate the pretty poetry, but not to bank on the substance. We simply do not feel how deeply and faithfully the Father values each single one of us.

The consequence of this lies heavy upon us when we turn to contemplate the passion of Jesus. For those who cannot appreciate how God the Father values us so much as to anoint us with Christ's blood— those cannot feel that Jesus' sufferings have anything to do with their own lives. They also cannot feel that their pains and sufferings have any value joined to Christ's. In the end, they can comprehend their own pains and sufferings only as inconveniences or as affronts to their (very questionable) value before God.

In this way, many of us are quite literally scandalized by God's continued refusal to ride roughshod into human history and end all our madnesses. We are scandalized that God continues infinitely patient, restrained so much beyond any measure we apply that we are constantly tempted to feel that He does not really care.

*"Simon, Simon!"* Jesus had exclaimed. *"Remember that Satan has asked for you to sift you all like wheat."*

*You all?* Then the sifting is not just for Peter. *"But I have prayed for you that your faith may never fail."*

Peter's faith did not fail, though for a brief moment his courage did. As Jesus turns to gaze at Peter and as the cock crows in the dawn of His last day, we turn to gaze at Him, because after all, every salvific argument is incarnate. All the others are nothing but wind.

-----------------------------------------------------------

In the end, our faith fails or does not fail if we can gaze on moiling humankind and truly hope that *those who hunger and thirst for what is right, shall be satisfied.*

In what senses can we say that Jesus, who hungered and thirsted for what is right more than anyone, has been satisfied?

When we gaze at the crucifix, how does it teach us that Jesus Christ is satisfied to have us as His own?

-----------------------------------------------------------

# Prayer

Lord Jesus Christ,
we find gazing on Your crucifixion
hard and full of distraction.

We do not comprehend how You came to this,
and if we understand a little bit
that we contribute to Your suffering,
You know that we do not right now understand it very much.

But one thing we do sense as You hang there, and know,
how total is Your love
for the Father whom You would not reject
for the Spirit whose guidance You trusted through the end
for Your Mother and the women, steady and faithful
for Your good friends, terrorized by Your loss of authority.

And we know among ourselves
how great a love it is that gives its life.

We are made mentally numb, good Lord and good brother,
by what was done to You, and by what keeps being done
to many, to the innocent, to children, to our own friends.

But we affirm before Your cross
hiding our face in our hands for shame and sorrow
that You have done well—that You have done very well
and we accept Your Holy Spirit to guide our selves
come whatever might come into our lives.

So Your victory may steadily grow greater and greater.

# 20. Hardy Perennials

*The teaching of Scripture [was] that He must rise from the dead.*

For more than a century now, rationalistic and liberal critics have been contending that Jesus did not really rise from the dead. They have argued variously that Jesus did not die, that the disciples stole the body, that Jesus' followers were hallucinating, or that they made up a myth. Even some faithful Christians have considered the Resurrection a metaphorical expression of what really happened, which is that Jesus lived on in His disciples' faith.

Some of these criticisms are not exactly new. In fact, they are a bit like the hardy perennials that fill the desert with fat leaves and stickers. Traces of three of them appear in the earliest teaching of the Good News.

The question, for instance, Did Jesus really die? That question lurks behind Christians' insistence that He was buried. The insistence shows up in a sentence Paul wrote to the Corinthians. In it, he evinces an unscriptural interest in the burial: *I taught you what I had been taught myself, namely that Christ died for our sins, in accordance with the Scriptures; that He was buried; and that He was raised to life on the third day, in accordance with the Scriptures.* Paul affirms that the dying and the rising are *in accordance with the Scriptures;* by omitting the phrase, he suggests that the burying is in accordance with the early concern to answer the false claim that Jesus had not really died.

Did the disciples steal the body, then? This criticism was voiced early, and recorded. Matthew reports the early Christian belief that enemies among the Jews had launched this canard, which was still current in Jerusalem in his own day. Everyone had to explain the empty tomb. But the disciples' belief was not in an empty tomb. In fact, they presumed that someone had taken the body when Magdalen found out that it was gone. They did not get beyond that. They were puzzled, and they would not at first believe anyone's stories about seeing Him.

Did they thereupon hallucinate? The question would be an obvious one, and the first to occur to a sane and sober citizen who had heard that other citizens were having breakfast with someone who just days ago had died dramatically in a public place. The disciples heard the accusation first from some of their own, who felt that the women had gone hysterical and were telling wild stories. They all learned soon enough. And then their preaching insisted on the physicalness of the risen Christ. Magdalen, for instance, did not cling to an hallucination. Peter preached that *we have eaten and drunk with Him after His resurrection from the dead.* Thomas in particular would remember that *He showed them His hands and feet,* and invited them to touch Him.

These three objections are hardy perennials which those who believe in Jesus' Resurrection have to reject just about every spring. They touch on details; newer objections are more sweeping.

Could the entire Jesus story be a fabrication? At the beginning of the 20th century, a famous study of the Greek god Orpheus proposed that the early Christians—consciously or unconsciously, who could say?—had shaped the story of Jesus' Resurrection after the beautiful legends about dying and rising gods like Adonis and Dionysus. When we think about it now, we may find it easier to believe that Jesus truly rose than that a group of illiterate Jews from Galilee adopted pagan myths so utterly alien to the Torah.

Anyhow, the harder anyone looked at the parallels, the less met the eye. The myths of Adonis and Dionysus tell about death in winter and the flowering life of springtime. Of this cycle, the disciples knew parallels in Jesus' life story: For instance, He had restored to earthly life the son of the widow of Naim, Jairus's daughter and Lazarus. Like winter-bare trees returning to full leaf, each of these would die again in the cycles of earth's life.

The history of Jesus, on the other hand, tells about the cycles of God's implosions into human history and about the whole of humankind's transcendence of its own mortality. In Jesus' story, seeding and harvesting are figures of speech and nothing more.

Can the Resurrection, though, have been just a figure of speech? Currently, some who believe in Jesus Christ are nonetheless skeptical about His Resurrection. The early Christians, they contend, had every reason to believe that Jesus had triumphed over death. He showed them His glory. But the disciples' problem was how to preach about that triumph, because the Hebrews did not believe in a "soul" that could live separated from the body. How could they make their compatriots understand that Jesus was alive now, in the present? Their solution was to express His triumph over death as a bodily resurrection. They accepted the tradition about the rising of the chosen on the last day, which had come down from the time of the Maccabees to the Pharisees, so they just moved Jesus' Resurrection into the present instead of waiting until the endtime. Jesus, therefore, had indeed been glorified, but spiritually; the disciples had had to affirm that He had risen already, physically.

If that is the tradition among Christ's disciples, then the Resurrection is indeed a figure of speech. So we have to ask of the tradition, Did something real happen to Jesus' body? If Jesus lives, did His body come back to earth's life or did it begin some new life?

What Peter preached from the first sermon, *what has been handed on to us,* is that the Carpenter from Nazareth was put to death and left in a hole in the rock. His friends found that hole empty a couple of mornings later and did not know what to make of it. They found out what to make of it when the Carpenter Himself came to tell them—or better, to show them—what they were to make of it.

So what has been handed on to us—to be believed by God's gift, or to be doubted in the world's wisdom—is that Jesus Christ lives, no longer confined by doors and walls, by hunger and tiredness, by the cycles of the sun and the moon. This is the real hardy perennial.

*Jesus Christ is the same today as He was yesterday and as He will be forever.*

------------------------------------------------------------

Had the very earliest disciples who did not visit with Him after His rising any different questions than we have?

What differences would there be in the worldview of those who do not expect resurrection and those who look forward to it?

May we dream of all things—the earth, the universes, every human person—made truly new? What are the values in that dream?

------------------------------------------------------------

# Prayer

Most glorious Lord of Life,
You freely put an end to Your sojourn on earth.

No one took it from You
as no one took Your body or squelched Your dreams.

For You chose to come again.

You have come not once but twice
to live in our humanness,
humbling Yourself to try again
what one attempt could not accomplish,
triumphing this time not for Yourself
but for us whom Your Father has given You for Your own.

For You have seized us in Your mighty power
and filled us with a Spirit of endurance
Who makes us boundlessly sure
that no matter how many bodies we plant
in this desert place of sundried desiring
we who live and move and have our being in You

will rise to hilarious gigs by angel choruses
and live with You and all the saints
hardily  perennial
in a world without end. Amen.

Right now, Lord, Amen.

We say Amen to that.

Amen.